Are We Nearly There Yet?

Also by Stephen Scourfield

Being Australian
North of Capricorn
Out Boating

Are We Nearly There Yet?

— *essays by* —

Stephen Scourfield

Particularly Australian Publishing

First published 1999 by Particularly Australian Publishing

Copyright © Stephen Scourfield 1999

National Library of Australia
Cataloguing-in-Publication data:
Scourfield, Stephen
Are We Nearly There Yet?

ISBN 0 909699 75 5

Printed by PK Print, Hamilton Hill, Western Australia.
Distributed by West Australian Newspapers, Osborne Park, Western Australia.
Colour scanning by West Australian Newspapers.

Are We Nearly There Yet?

"A reference to humankind's position
environmentally, culturally, technologically
and emotionally.

A reference to my position
personally and as a writer.

A memory from every car trip a
child ever took.

Are we nearly there yet?

In some ways we are frighteningly close,
in others we have barely started."

— *Stephen Scourfield*

PHOTOGRAPHIC ESSAY
By Stephen Scourfield

FRONT COVER (clockwise from top left):
Fossil stromatolites in the Cradle of Life; Ingebong Hill, in the Western Australian desert; gorge in Karijini National Park; Australian urban wrought iron "lace work"; dawn river at Nullagine, Pilbara; classical guitar by luthier Scott Wise; bush home, Australia; canvas camping swags.

BACK PAGE (clockwise from top left):
Trees on Wilson Inlet, Denmark, Western Australia; lake at Karri Valley Resort, Pemberton; winter lake on Canning Stock Route; aerial photography at Port Hedland; Cape Leveque, north of Broome; water and pier pylons; Lasseter, the author's Australian kelpie-dingo cross; boat at Coral Bay, North-West Cape; author in the bush.

Following page: Wall of the old Roebourne jail, in the North-West of Western Australia. Childhood pictures of the author (above, with sister) by his mother, Shirley. Boots artwork by Virginia Ward.

THE ESSAYS

Foreword

ESSAYS ARE LESS ABOUT DESTINATIONS than journeys.

The best allow a form to develop naturally, moving from one thought to another, unhurried and unprescribed. They have nothing so miserly in mind as a point and a mission to deliver it; they have, instead, an idea, a thought, and an inclination to explore it.

The best essays are unlikely hybrids of memory, observation, analysis and reportage.

They are, perhaps, a little undisciplined – not above taking liberties with style and structure if it helps communicate a thought.

They are intimate in ways beyond many other literary forms.

Are We Nearly There Yet? is a very personal collection of essays. In part because much of the subject matter is autobiographical, but more importantly because there is never any doubt that there is a single mind behind them. They are united by perspective and voice, and driven forward by the momentum of exploration.

Angela Wellington
Editor

Introduction

TAPED TO THE WALL of my office is a dog-eared cartoon. It is quite old now. You can see it has been moved from office to office by the number of pin holes in each corner, the Blutack stains showing through and, as a final desperation, the torn-off corners where tape has been used and the cartoon ripped down to be moved.

Doubtless it will one day be replaced by a photocopy of itself (complete with holes, stains and the shading of ragged corners).

It features a series of small drawings of a glob-like character. He is sitting in front of a doctor's desk, saying: "Help me doctor, I've got a book inside me."

The doctor replies: "Most people have a book in them. Perhaps I can refer you to a publisher."

"I don't want to become a ... WRITER!" the character insists. "NO! I don't want it published – I want it surgically removed."

The doctor says he doesn't think that will work. "We must

1

learn acceptance. We are born, we live and then, sadly, we must write." The reply: "It seems so unfair."

And so it is. At night, I will often have to get up again after half an hour in bed. For in the dark I can fool myself that, in the morning, I will be able to remember a good line of poetry that comes to me – but inevitably a second follows. "Yes, I can make two," I think. Then a third line. But by the time the fourth comes tacking in, white words streaming over the constantly blue ocean of near-sleep, I know I'm dead meat. The light has to go on. ("Damn.")

I don't keep a notebook and pen by my bed as it reminds me of people who write down dreams. I get up and do it properly, and inevitably continue working on the piece until it comes to some conclusion – either a point where I can happily leave it as a "work in progress" (with as much chance as the house renovation of being finished) or complete.

I have made my living from writing – it has been my life – for more than 20 years now, and have occasionally been asked: "How do you write?" The first time, I groped around for words which now seem like platitudes. From my soul, my heart, my brain, my spirit, my sense of the beautiful or ridiculous. "No, I meant which sort of computer have you got?"

The type of computer is, of course, totally irrelevant. And originally I would answer that the actual medium was irrelevant too. But, as a writer, I try to maintain the flexibility to change my mind. (I have another cutting taped to the office wall which argues the case for "consistency of opinion being a sign of small-mindedness".) And, in this case, I have.

The medium of writing does affect the style – perhaps even the content – of a piece. A laptop allows a faster, smoother flow of ideas (and seamless editing). A foolscap, spiral bound book encourages a casual "notebook feel" to prose and good, long lines of poetry. A tiny, scrappy pocket book might lead to staccato style, or short, pithy, more pointed poetry.

2

Bruce Chatwin's moleskin-covered pocket books are legendary. When travelling, he took a good store of the books, bought from a particular place in France, and kept all his thoughts, notes, diagrams and early writings carefully in them.

You get very used to a particular set of conditions, and familiarity makes them less distracting. You focus on the words, not the typing, longhand or shorthand.

§   §   §   §   §

It strikes me that a good, rewarding read ... a good essay ... a good mix of information and entertainment ... is something like a good meal. We don't eat just for sustenance (although there can be no doubt that if we did, the planet would be better off). We eat for entertainment.

We might reflect on that "great meal" last week. There were interesting people round the table, the conversation was spontaneous and textured, touching on the engaging or controversial, dipping into the amusing. It was a night to remember. How was the food? Oh, it was OK. We think. And what was it? We might not be able to recall its exact components, or ouline its makeup of carbohydrates or vitamins. But somehow that doesn't matter. It was a great meal.

Perhaps only once a year, I read something that really surprises me, just because it is so good. It might be an in-depth analysis of how to strip a tractor gearbox, or a piece on flower arranging, or a profile of a little-known mathematics lecturer. Something that I have no particular interest in.

I scan over the first few words. Then the strangest thing happens – the next time I lift my eyes, it is because I have reached the final full point. I have been swept along by the words, just for the joy of reading. I may not be able to tell you the ingredients, just that it was a great piece of writing and reading it was, in itself, an enjoyable thing to do.

§   §   §   §   §

There are three phases to producing a book. First there is the idea. I love having ideas to carry around in my head – projects I can drag out and play with in airport lounges between flights, or on nights when I can't sleep, perhaps when I'm away on a writing assignment. I like to allow them to gestate, to fill them out, to give them time to prove themselves.

The second phase is the actual work of writing. I include in that the research, perhaps the travelling, the notemaking, the outlining, then the actual work of sitting down at a keyboard, producing words.

I love both of these phases, though the second less than the first. If we are born to do one thing in particular, then they are, I feel sure, what I was born to do.

The last phase is the publishing. The work has to be physically produced in a presentable form.

I used to think this phase totally irrelevant – that the first two should be the sole motive and motivation for writing. But the editor of this book advised me: "It's ALL about getting it out. It's ALL about publishing." And I've changed my mind on this too, and now agree with her. (Though it still seems to me philosophically wrong that the act of publishing should be the motive.)

The endeavour must be to produce work of great quality. "Let the quality of the work speak for you," a good friend once wisely counselled. It is the best advice I can think of.

Demolishing the Suburbs

It was a pretty, ordinary house.
(Pretty and Ordinary, that is.)
And then it was gone.

NO-ONE REALLY NOTICED the house, because it was so much in the style of the old Australian suburb. White, balanced. The front door in the centre, a room either side (as shown by their perfectly matching sash windows). Two chimneys. Divisible down the middle: a reflection of itself.

No-one noticed the house, and that was its greatest attribute. Its great contribution to the suburb. It was a house the way others were. And that's what helped to make the area what it is, and what drew to it the type of people who cluster here. Not an Architect's

Statement. More a classic house the way a child might have drawn one. A simple place to live. A home for a family and for generations.

The house was set in the middle of its corner block. It was a quiet place, with the ocean back over its shoulder, a small park opposite.

There was no fence around the front yard, where the remnants of a landscaped garden presented themselves as clues, glimpsing through the long grass. A dogrose. A rangy bougainvillea. Rocks that may once have encircled a small pond. Someone – perhaps many people – had spent time in the garden, back through the house's life. They gardened the way people did in their day. Their tastes were typical. They put in a lemon tree. A frangipani, since grown enormous. A row of Rottnest pines which topped the sky-line and became a landmark. More unusually, a loquat.

The wooden shed was falling down on one side, but that was its charm. If you were brave enough to sneak a look through the windows, you would have seen an old child's bike, chainless, the chrome bars pitted with rust. No seat. A few golf clubs stuck in a beige vinyl bag, laced over with cobwebs. One sticking out, reveal-ing a wooden shaft. Two wooden and warped tennis racquets hang-ing on a nail. Stringless. The rest was hard to make out – just a dark tangle of the discards of maybe three decades.

In its last years, the house had been rented out, and a succes-sion of young geologists moved through. Sometimes there were two in the house, sometimes three, sometimes four. It was often hard to tell. They were away in the field for long spells, so some-times the place seemed empty, sometimes full.

The geologists always invited the neighbours to their backyard parties, where a couple of dozen people would congregate around the shopping trolley that was now a barbecue. There were plenty of cold beers and conversation. The parties might go on until 3am, but the noise was never threatening. By then, it would be muted voic-es with occasional bursts of appreciative laughter. They had dragged in a felled electricity pole when the suburb's power lines went underground, and used this as a bench. Here they sat, storytelling. It reminded the old man over the back laneway of his days in the bush.

The geologists liked a good time, but they had a depth too. I used to regularly see one involved in some complicated conversation with the little boy from next door. Perhaps they would be sitting on the back step. Perhaps working at some small job in the yard. Perhaps washing an old car on the verge. More likely they would be sitting on the decrepit vinyl lounge suite on the front verandah, discussing the world. For once, the child would do more listening than talking, as he sat and pushed his fingers into the splits and cracks. (In one of the greatest Australian traditions, the lounge suite had been hauled out on to the verandah, after it had served a life inside.)

There had never been a driveway. Never a garage. Holdens and utes were strewn along the verge, or on the front lawn. Never in the same place, or the same order. Abandoned more than parked.

Then, one day, the Mercedes appeared, though no For Sale sign had gone up. It cruised past, shark-like. Rounded the corner. Cruised back past a couple of minutes later. No-one got out or spoke. But soon the block was surveyed, and pegs with bright pink plastic ribbons were hammered in.

They used to knock houses down, now they dismantle them. It didn't take long. The house was deconstructed, and its parts carted away. The sandstone walls were pushed flat in a swirling storm of dust, which then settled in piles, waiting for the sea breeze. The plumbing pipes spouted water for a while, as the building finally bled to death.

Only the loquat tree was left standing, and that because a neighbour had cajoled the man in the crane to lift it over the fence into her garden (where it eventually died). The others were strewn around the site like broken bodies. The weathered wooden fence went too: a flourescent plastic barrier mesh hung in its place.

Then the rubble was gone, and it was all gone. The little boy next door called it The Great Sandy Desert. And in The Great Sandy Desert, the boy's mother found a cup decorated with a rooster wearing a yellow shirt and blue trousers, holding playing cards. She found an old marble, swirled red and yellow, which she gave to her son.

The block has since been subdivided into two. It didn't surprise me. That's what has been happening everywhere. That's how our old suburbs have been changing and our lifestyles changing with them. Perhaps we don't have time for gardening and proper houses now, or choose to use our time in other ways and think we are busier. Perhaps we are losing some of the skills of looking after our homes and gardens. Simple carpentry and repairs. Fixing up a fence. Not in slick little units.

Perhaps we now prefer to be entertained.

Subdivision changes the way we live. With more people in the same space, it increases the social pressure. But I'm sure a good environmental case can be made for subdivision, as it helps to reduce the pace of urban sprawl. Armies of roofs marching north, marching south. Gobbling up land, and covering bush with hard surface. Replacing native species with garden varieties. Changing water run-offs: a new car park covers a natural spring in the hills and bitumen haemorrhages pure, sweet fresh water through widening cracks each autumn.

The social effects of Infill or the environmental effects of Urban Sprawl? That's the conundrum.

§ § § § §

The simple facia of the white house still haunts me. I have been struggling to put my finger on exactly why. Not nostalgia. It was just that it was there, and it had been there a long time, and it was fine. But it — and its values and the lifestyle it represented — were too easily discarded for money. Perhaps in other suburbs it wouldn't have been so quick and easy.

And the units replacing it? Well, the plans show them to be just like modern units anywhere. And so the character of a place changes into just so much fast food.

*A burger's
a burger's
a burger.*

§   §   §   §   §

Do we still have homes in the sense that our grandparents did? A friend recently bought an aviary. It was quite cheap and pre-assembled, but it was made of tin, and shiny and nasty. Despite this, I found myself thinking of getting one too. Then I remembered the story of another friend's grandfather.

The old man had built an aviary in his backyard, for his son, who was then in his late teens (but still called Boy, as he was until he was a Man and eventually dropped dead in his early 50s of a heart attack).

The aviary was very big. First Grandad had marked out the area with pegs, then he'd made a concrete pad to stop rats digging in. He had carried bags of concrete and sand down the yard — slung in his arms, fingers locked underneath — from the trailer behind his old Holden out the front of the house. It had been a baking hot day. Half way through the afternoon he'd taken off his blue checked shirt and worked in his white singlet. The children had never seen him in public in his singlet before, never seen the flabbiness of the back of his arms or their whiteness. He looked like a baby, all white in white. He looked like them. They could smell his sweat.

When he had put up the aviary's vertical poles, he'd called Grandma, and all the kids hanging round the place, to come and help. She came from the kitchen, in the apron which she invariably wore. Clapping the flour from her hands. The kids dumped their tatty bikes all over the lawn, which was his pride.

Grandad had lifted the poles like cabers, fingers locked, and dropped them into the holes he had dug. He packed them out with concrete and everyone was told to hold them still, perfectly vertical, for what had seemed an interminable length of time. The poles were of tall, green pine and you could almost smell their arsenic soak. They waved around, describing shaky arcs and figure-eights in the air and the grandson felt quite panic stricken about the effect this would be having on their concrete footing. Everyone tried to hold them still, bending heads under the sun now directly above, squinting eyes. But then Mother had started giggling (the only time he can remember this), and they'd all started giggling, and it was hopeless.

Grandad had later come up with a system of garden twine and pegs, to hold the poles still. He joined them with horizontal pieces of wood and then tapped wire mesh over the whole lot, with little arched pins.

My friend's memory of all this is quite clear, and the description of the aviary is perfectly accurate. It was a feature of the family home for three decades and I knew it too. It had a double door system to prevent the birds escaping – you stepped through the first door with the second shut, closed the first behind you, then opened the second.

The interior of the aviary was exotic – quite another world. You could see the normal world through the mesh and on occasions make verbal contact, but it was very far away and quite irrelevant. Inside the aviary there was the scrunch of seed under your feet, the whirr and buzz of wings, flashing colours, the smell of bird dust, and magic. As a youngster, I would happily sit in there for hours, among the branches and white-specked bushes.

Boy only ever wanted budgerigars (though at times he was pressured to have more exceptional birds). At first he only wanted them in their native green and yellow colours. They flew together, coherent as a storm. A flash of green and gold, fluttering across the aviary. A flag.

Eventually he expanded into other colours, breeding birds and exhibiting them. He built a shed on to the side of the aviary, and cut a keyhole between the two, for the birds to get to their rows of perches. In the evening, they sat like a musical manuscript and gossiped.

He covered one wall with nesting boxes, which he made himself. It all sat on a concrete pad.

My friend had been in the kitchen with Grandma (who was teaching him, as a teenager, to make a simple sponge cake) when he heard the car pull up with the old trailer behind. Boy carried the bags of concrete for the shed down the yard with his fingers locked underneath. Halfway through, after the teenager had clapped the flour off his hands and run to help, Boy had taken off his shirt and worked in his singlet, his strong brown arms muscular and taut.

The aviary was a landmark ... a touchstone ... of many childhoods, though after Boy married and moved out it stood largely empty and rubbish had gathered in the shed. Rusty old bikes. Stringless wooden tennis rackets, warped and delaminating. When they eventually knocked down the house, they had flattened the aviary too. The timber poles lay around like bodies. Boy had plumbed in a tap, and its severed pipe spouted water for a while, as the place finally bled to death.

Anthem in England

AT NINE O'CLOCK, IN STREETS still light, my evening beat stretches out around England's houses, to the cacophony of television soapies and quizzes and animal shows leaking from open windows through the muggy summer heat. Some children play in pocket-handkerchief front gardens, or on the road. Others unable to sleep despite heavy curtains.

It stretches past housing estates poured hard over meadows, displacing skylarks.

How many times, as a child, did I lie on my back in meadow grass to watch a lark high and bouncing and singing to heaven, then dropping into the soft, green, flower-rashed eiderdown – to race to her nest a distance off, so that I didn't know where it was. But I did. And carefully avoided it.

This was before the cancerous tumours of housing stuck sticky to cities and towns and villages, endangering the larks and swamping Norman churches. Making them incongruous centrepieces rather than simply part of everyday life.

The roads then were empty. Now they snake colourful with nose-to-tail cars, but still burrow between the hedgerows, high with brambles and dogrose, and tinted by the new cream blush of sweet meadow in flower. Alive with bird conversation.

England looks fine in summer, and parallel to its modern face, I still see other clear flashes of the place where I grew up 30 years ago. The change is real, but only physical. It is paint on this canvas, but the canvas is unchanged.

The spine of the Malvern Hills – framed below by copse and field and lane, and above by hot blue sky and marshmallow cloud – remains more familiar than my own. It is the backbone of my childhood. I can close my eyes and trace every lump and bump and innuendo, and know they are precisely the same shapes and heights as when I was a child.

Today the hills are a source of memory and nostalgia, and a fresh-born wonder at their beauty (and geological and human history). Then they were an adventure playground, with very specific sites for very specific games. The Water Quarry, Red Bum slide, The Climbing Quarry.

But strongest in my memory is the Amphitheatre. High above the world, which spread around our feet (the streets like rows of theatre stalls), we would spend the mornings of our school holidays making up and rehearsing plays – to perform to the grownups when they walked along the crests after work, with a vacuum flask and biscuits, to join us for the early evening performance. They were an appreciative audience, and enthusiastic clappers.

We would all walk back together, hand in hand, the children breaking away to run, wheeling like Spitfires or ponies, to my grandparents' cottage, perched over the jigsaw of English countryside facing the Black Mountains beyond. The smell of Grandpa's pipe smoke. The late ziz of flies and the swish of bracken fronds. At nine o'clock, on paths still light, our evening beat spread through the high countryside of England, to the cacophony of wind and insects, and our own conversation and laughter.

Many Kinds of Freedom

MY DAD LEFT WHEN I was nine years old – though, curiously, it was us who piled into the little hire car and drove away. My 12-year-old sister, white with anger, stared out of the side window, jaw set, possessions piled in her lap. My four-year old brother, too young to gauge what was going on, bored before we got to the end of the road, was rocking violently in his safety seat, covered with toys.

Mother at the wheel, concentrated on the road – trying, I suppose, to block everything else out. Occasionally she would turn to my sister. "Are you all right?" Turning back when there was no reply, watching the teenager swallow her pain to a place so deep, I thought it would never dissolve.

The only person I don't really remember is me. I guess I just sat there, piled up too, watching the scenery parade past as we drove from city to country.

It had been coming for some time. Dad was always busy, always at work, never there for us. He only called in, it seemed to me, to have us expelled from the house while he worked in silence at the big lounge room table, and to argue with my mother. So it's strange that the day he told me that he and my mother were parting, he had been teaching me how to throw a javelin in the back yard. (He was a javelin champion who had earned my undying awe for once pinning together the legs of an umpire. They had trouble getting him into the ambulance.)

We were sitting together under a tree, which was strange too. I can't remember many other moments of physical contact with him. I remember a feeling of falling when he told me, as if gravity was pulling the life out of me.

My dad got to see us once a month, but those Sundays were disastrous. He would drive a couple of hours from the city to pick us up. The day was invariably rainy, and we would then spend the next few hours moping around looking for something to do, getting wet, sitting in the steamy car, or a cafe, making difficult conversation punctuated by awkward silences. My memory of my sister during those Sunday visits is of her still staring out of the window, white-faced, with that set jaw. (Even if she doesn't share the memory.)

One Sunday I told him this didn't seem to be working. We didn't see him again. (I now know the cost to him of staying away, which he believed to be the best thing for us.)

When I was in my twenties, I met my father again. My brother had changed his surname to that of my stepfather, my sister had her own family by now. My father had remarried and I managed to move between the two families and our friendship grew.

Then he got cancer. Myeloma. Cancer of the bone marrow, or

something. He was steady on the phone when he told me, entirely positive. And that's how he stayed for the next four years, until he died.

We lived through protein level counts, pain and vomiting, hope and tasteless jokes, remission and the devastation of seeing the damned thing start up again.

At the end, I sat by his hospital bedside for three days, watching him struggle. Watching his silent resistance, anger and frustration. On the third morning a floor-cleaner barged through the door, took one look at him and backed out again. "Sorry. I'll come back tomorrow." Then he died.

My father was old-fashioned, very conservative. During the funeral, my main worry was that he would somehow know he was being cremated by a female vicar wearing scuffed turquoise sandals, knee-length hold-up stockings and a short skirt. If, by any chance, he wasn't totally dead in there, I knew this would finish him off.

My brother came, and put his shoulder to the coffin. My sister stayed away.

Funerals are by nature emotional affairs, but even by my clouded judgment, this one was particularly so. The terrible sense of loss was palpable in the church. A good man had gone, and community groups were there to mourn the loss. The last four years of my father's life, during his cancer, were undeniably his best. He worked to the end, always remained cheery, became involved with charities, made new friends. Most of the people he met during those last four years didn't even know he had cancer. Those that did joined a common refrain: "He never complained."

Later that evening, I was sitting quietly with my stepmother of 25 years. I mentioned this. "It's amazing how many people said: 'He never complained'. Everyone really."

"You know WHY he never complained don't you?" she replied. I didn't. She told me that late at night a few weeks before … a long night of pain … he had told her that he was glad to have the cancer. It had made him happy. It was his penance, his payment for leaving his first family. It had lifted the guilt from his shoulders. It was his "just desserts". And with it, he found relief and a new, if short, life.

I will never get over the sadness that my father had spent the majority of his life racked by such guilt and suffering. Frankly, I generally don't fall in with the philosophy that "you get the illness you deserve", or even give yourself an illness. But I know my father gave himself cancer, and I know he didn't deserve it.

§   §   §   §   §

Death brings a time of memory, and now I remember clearly that the only time I smelt the Old Man, I was about five years old and we were on the back lawn in Kent and he was teaching me how to rugby scrum.

He was hunkered down low under a blue English sky and our shoulders were locked together. His cheek was scratchy and he had that sort of musty man smell. I was quite conscious of the fact that I had never smelt that scent before, and I was distracted by the notion that I had really never felt his skin either.

We had already done the brief run-through. It is hard to imagine how a five-year-old would grasp exactly when a scrum is called for in rugby union, but the rules had been duly and precisely outlined, as was his way.

Then we got down to it and shoved and grunted. We bonded like two men should. Until sweat was running from the end of his sideburns and my knees were green from the grass.

From that day on, rugby union was an unfailing connection between us. A touchstone. We would talk for hours about the technicalities and intricacies of a particular game. Talk about it as if it were a gearbox, the contents of which we were carefully and clinically stripping apart, cog by cog. We would wash these parts off, lay them out on the table, seriously study the detail of them.

Life takes people apart too, and life brought me to Australia, nearly 20,000 kilometres from the strange, stiff and unhappy little country I was born in and which didn't fit me. The Old Man was still there, along with the rest of the family, and he got the cancer. There were good days and bad days and worse days, when he made very little sense at all. Days when the morphine stopped it hurting, but he made even less sense. He was good at making them all sound the same on the phone. You couldn't pick one from the other.

One day we were discussing a particular rugby game in a rugby union world cup. I had been in Australia a couple of years and was avidly following the series, as was he. When we had exhausted the subject of the state of his cancer – a disease which dominates every conversation around it – we both fell back, with some relief, on the previous night's match.

We started stripping down that gearbox, but the Old Man didn't make much sense. He would make some rash and quite wrong statement about the fullback, or the weight of the pack, or the inability to move the ball out along the line, or the wrong choice of lineout lengths, and I'd let it go. (Somehow you can't tell someone dying of cancer that he's an idiot.)

That was, until he made a rash and, again, quite wrong statement about the wing being ineffective, unresponsive, slow and, quite frankly, useless. "How can you say that about Campese? I just think you're wrong."

"Who?"

"Campese. He played a blinder."

"I wasn't talking about him. I was talking about OUR winger."

I had watched every game the Australian Wallaby team had played. For me, they were US, they were WE, they were OUR. The Old Man, of course, had been talking about the England team. We had been completely at cross-purposes for 20 minutes.

This was a pivotal moment in my life. It was the moment I realised I was an Australian. I had changed sides. Not only was I unable to name more than a couple of England players, but I had no interest whatsoever in them. I was only interested in Wallaby games, Wallaby results and Wallaby fortunes. (This was just as well, because they won the world cup.)

Since then I have called myself an Australian, travelled as an Australian, been proud of being an Australian. I have felt a sense of belonging. Cut me open and you will see that the colour of my soul has changed from the green of an English meadow to the red-ochre of the Outback's pindan soil.

I think my father was what I would have been if I hadn't come here. And I think I am what he wanted to be.

§　　§　　§　　§　　§

It is more than two weeks since I arrived back home, with my dead father's ashes in a black plastic container in my backpack. The immigration officer didn't know quite what to do. Anything to declare? Yes. My dad. He peeled the lid off, hung his sharp index finger over the grey dust, threatening to push it in and swirl it around. "Don't rearrange him." He thought better of it, and closed the lid again.

The container stood on a shelf, out of the way. I didn't know what to do with its contents, but felt that some moment would arrive.

It has. Tonight.

It is 2am and I have woken from a deep sleep. For no apparent reason. I am calm, rested, totally awake, and completely aware that this is the moment. I know where to go and what to do. In fact, not only have I woken knowing that the ashes must go to the river, but I know exactly where. Not somewhere close, or even places I had walked with my father when he visited. Not the spots that are important to me, or where I have walked the dog every morning or picnicked.

I must go to the other side – the south side – of the river, and launch from a quiet little beach near a jetty.

I wake up just knowing all this.

I dress quietly and carefully, putting on only things that I really like to wear. Then I go outside. I hadn't realised it was a full moon, but there is an eerie blue light and complete stillness. More strangely there is a thick, still fog. Not mist – deep, white fog sitting like cotton wool, so I can't even see the end of the driveway. I have literally never seen anything like it before in Perth.

I carefully lift out my favourite kayak and strap it to the roof bars. Then I pick out my favourite paddle. Everything is done quietly. There is an almost dreamlike quality to the flow of things.

With the ashes, I drive slowly, picking my way along a road which is mostly obliterated by fog – a London "pea-souper" from a Sherlock Holmes story.

Unloading the kayak and preparing to launch it, I am struck by the complete stillness of the water. Not just surface calm, but the body of water itself is absolutely motionless. I study the edge of the water and see no movement against the sand.

I am standing in a strange pall of white light. The full moon is above me, and it shines down a white tunnel of fog to where I stand. It's like something out of a Monty Python film — I expect God's big, pink cartoon hand to reach down and grab me at any moment.

This vision adds some levity to a sombre moment. No — that's an exaggeration. It isn't really sombre. I am warm, feeling quiet and rested, and I am completely at peace with what I am doing and must do. I feel deliciously happy, really.

I put the black container next to my kayak, in the white tunnel of light, and ease into the boat. It fits snugly, and adds to my comfort and security. I have been sliding into these things all my life, and I feel at home.

I push up the sleeves of my old jumper to prevent the cuffs getting wet. It's the last jumper my mother knitted me before the arthritis in her hands made her stop.

All I can think of is Hiawatha, and Henry Wadsworth Longfellow's words, with their perfect rhythme. Hiawatha, the great young American Indian leader, sailing his birch canoe out over the waters when his time to die has come ...

On the shore stood Hiawatha,
Turned and waved his hand in parting;
On the clear and luminous water
Launched his birch canoe for sailing,
From the pebbles of the margin
Shoved it forth into the water;
Whispered to it, "Westward! westward!"
And with speed it darted forward.

How I have loved that story. Hiawatha's honest love for Minnehaha, and his final, private journey. It shows acceptance and strength. Balance and peace. I admire it.

I paddle out slowly, the plastic bottle resting on the spray deck over my thighs. Only now do I have a sense of goodbye. I try not to make any sound with the blades, sliding them straight down into the water, trying not to make ripples.

The fog is just as thick in the middle of the river – or what I guess to be the middle – and the tower of white light remains above me. I find it strange that this act should be spotlit.

I expect the ashes to float, like lily leaves, but I start to pour and whoosh, they are gone, heavy as gravel. I see only a milky stain heading for the bottom.

And the people from the margin
Watched him floating, rising, sinking,
Till the birch canoe seemed lifted
High into that sea of splendour,
Till it sank into the vapors
Like the new moon, slowly, slowly
Sinking in the purple distance.

It occurs to me that I have been sitting there for a while, and I know the motions of a boat well enough to realise I have turned around. In fact, I am totally lost. Sitting in the broad middle of the Swan River, completely isolated, completely unaware of exactly where I am, or which way I should head.

The comforting thing about rivers is that if you head in any direction, you will eventually get somewhere (presuming you can paddle straight). And so I set off, trying to perfectly measure left and right strokes so that the kayak moves in a straight line. It's not something you ever think about, with the benefit of normal sight. It's an interesting exercise and it amuses me enough to distract me.

I am not sure how long I have been paddling. It seems like a long time. Suddenly, out of the fog, there appear boats tied up in pens, less than three metres in front of me. I frantically back-paddle and stop. Considering I left the little beach just upstream from the jetty at Point Walter, I initially have no idea whether the boats are at Royal Flying Squadron Yacht Club, Claremont Yacht Club or Royal Freshwater Bay Yacht Club.

But the style of boat and pens makes me believe it is Claremont. I paddle along in front of the boats until I am sure. Yes, I am sure. To get directly back to Point Walter would mean paddling diagonally back across a wide section of the river.

I am not convinced I have mastered the art of paddling completely straight.

I decide to creep around the edge, and head left.

It is hard following the bank when you can't see it. I try to keep out far enough to have enough water to paddle, then the bank peels away and vanishes. It takes a long time to crawl my way around to Freshie. Perhaps an hour.

I set off towards Point Walter but after a long time paddling, haven't found it. Since its long, sandy finger is pointing directly towards me, this means I have missed to either the left or the right. Which? Which direction should I head to find it? If I head the wrong way, I could be out here all night. As I paddle on, trying to decide, I run into the end of it.

I follow its shore back to the jetty, bumping my paddle on the sandy, sometimes rough bottom, the kayak dragging its backside in shallow water. Eventually – and only when I am right on top of them – I see the lights at the end of the jetty.

A week later, I set out on my regular Wednesday evening paddle with a mate. We paddle out from near Claremont Yacht Club towards the end of the spit, on our way to Fremantle.

"Look at your boat. Look at the wake," he says. "Look at that colour." We have both been paddling for years, seen all sorts of colours. But nothing like this. More than phosphorescence, more like backlit green toothpaste. We look around but there's no obvious light source, nothing different to any other week we paddle over this spot.

Then it goes.

On the way back from Fremantle, in the same spot, the boats are lit by the same green.

I once called my friend a cynic and he said, no he was a sceptic. Another time I called him a sceptic and he said, no he's a cynic. Perhaps he's both. Certainly he's very logical, and prone to savagely dissecting nonsense.

He's never mentioned the light since. Certainly never mauled the memory with his biting little sense of humour. I don't think he ever will.

A Dormant Nature

THE SIMPLEST THINGS CAN DREDGE up parts of you concealed in your genes. A piece falling from a bedroom ceiling can add a quite eerie dimension to a newly-acquired love of gardening.

Like many people, I had always thought of gardening as a series of jobs that simply had to be done when they could no longer be avoided. Maintenance work, not something constructive, not the creation of an aesthetic environment.

The big garden around my home in an "old" Australian suburb has many tall trees, interesting nooks and crannies, and reminders of the keen gardeners during its 60-year life. Some obviously put in a lot of time and effort. I once spent a weekend clearing a mountain of ivy to find an ancient rockery and waterfall underneath.

The problem, eventually, was that the garden had turned into landscaping's equivalent of those ghastly, sprawling "greatest hits over the decades" music compilations.

Whatever the fashion, it was applied – in great quantity. There was a four metre by three metre, 1970s brick barbecue with a huge crematorium-like chimney. What seemed like hectares of stone paving, laid at different times and in varying colours. Built-up borders, girthed by railway sleepers. A quartz rockery, old fences, newer fences, a fish pond with a little stone bridge too narrow for a foot, an old brick letterbox stand. There were strange, spiky succulents from Africa, a huge jacaranda, eucalypts, tea-trees, a 10 metre rubber tree, a couple of large (occasionally-flowering) cacti, a tangle of bougainvillea, wisteria, and lemon, orange and mandarin trees.

After probably half a dozen or more keen gardeners have done their dash you have, well, a dog's breakfast.

Earlier in the garden's history, the people involved clearly had more time available for maintenance – or perhaps their psyche was simply more attuned to it. One modern working man simply couldn't keep it going, and with any available time spent on maintenance, there was no chance of improvement.

While the backyard had degenerated into something not to be proud of, the front was a positive disgrace. It was originally just a huge swathe of thatched lawn, on a slope. Then the reticulation packed up. The lawn died. The years passed.

Soil erosion was a problem until the dandelions moved in. (Not ordinary dandelions, but big, tough clumps any kid with a mountain bike would love to jump over – with tap roots you'd fight for, and live on, if you were in the desert.)

I tried to convince visitors that "clump planting" was all the rage. They really should try it. No-one believed me.

Then the dandelions started forming seed-bearing heads, waist-high and almost the size of tennis balls. I could see the neighbours eyeing them fearfully, waiting for the first vague breath of wind, praying it wouldn't be in their direction.

One evening, it rained and softened the soil. I went out at

11pm and spent several hours pulling them all up, stacking them in giant heaps, too embarrassed to do it in the light.

The next day the phone rang. It was a friend from a couple of streets away. She cut to the chase. "I'm ringing to complain about your front yard."

"AH-HA," I said gleefully. "You can't. I pulled out the dandelions last night."

"That's what I'm complaining about. They were a landmark. I used to bring overseas visitors sightseeing there. What am I going to do with them now?"

The dandelions were gone, but the front yard now reminded me of a film I once saw of the early days of the gold rush in inland Australia, the landscape pockmarked with miners' craters and "rabbit holes".

Things had gone from bad to disgraceful. Then the piece fell from the bedroom ceiling, and everything changed.

If the garden had shown the ravages of neglect, the house wasn't much better. I could always attempt to explain away the wall cracks by attributing them to the Meckering earthquake (though it was some decades before), there were no excuses for the old concrete tile roof. Whoever came up with the idea of using concrete tiles for a roof must have had a strange and particularly unpleasant sense of humour. At various times over the years the roof had been "restored", "renovated" and "revived", though this had never seemed to include stopping it leaking. At the last count, there were still 20 broken tiles and enough light to read a newspaper in the loft.

There had been no point in trying to do anything with the garden when, eventually, the day would come when 10 tonnes of concrete tiles would rain upon it. And that day had come. There was no point repairing the back bedroom ceiling until the roof was fixed, and so it was. Beautifully. The dark green corrugated tin roof looked splendid. A finial was added. The house was painted, heritage-red trim added. It looked damned pretty. It enthused me. With a white picket fence splitting the slope out front, a real garden suddenly looked possible.

In came Bob in his bobcat, with trucks to take the old gardens away. Easier said than done – under the barbecue, a half metre-thick poured concrete raft, the fish pond built like a testing tank for ocean liners. Scattered deep in the soil throughout the garden, marbles of different colours and sizes, strangely echoing childhood games. I carefully kept every one.

The backyard was planted with native trees and shrubs and completely mulched. "What, like scrub?" a friend observed. Well, yes, just like scrub really. Like being in the Australian bush.

With Bernie strutting around in charge and labourer Jane mixing concrete, the front became a cottage garden – terraced, with recycled brick retaining walls, circular brick paving, reticulation, fresh soils, fertilisers, plenty of mulch and borders of native plants.

I became obsessed. I started listening to radio gardening programs (adding it to my obsessive preference for footy match wireless commentaries over watching a game on TV). Someone gave me a book about classic gardens. All the old women gardeners looked like my maternal grandmother – the same distracted expression, the same impression that they could converse more easily with plants than people, the same stoop and battered white hat.

When I started cleaning out the bedroom, ready for a new ceiling, I found a box of photographs. Among them, a curled black-and-white image of a five-year-old, squinting in the sun, under a black velvet riding hat, at an early horse riding lesson. My little legs stick out virtually horizontal, having very little grip and very little bearing on where the pony was going.

The great event at horse riding lessons was Riding Out. Every now and then, we would be taken away from the arena, the smell of sawdust and the safety of enclosing fences, to ride in open areas. Riding Out was a nerve wracking time for a five-year-old (as a 35-

year-old, I recall, nothing had changed much).

A memory as clear as the smell of the warm horses came back to me. I could see our stooped, old grandmother – visiting us for summer holidays – in her battered white hat following our little Riding Out party round the country town's streets, with a bucket and shovel. As a child, one of the earliest things I learnt was that there is nothing, but nothing, as good for roses as the sweet, steaming product of a riding lesson.

My sister and I used to die. We'd come back with sore legs from continually kicking our steeds on, trying to get away from the spectre-like figure following behind. We never did. Invariably she would end up just a few metres behind us as we turned back in through the gate to the stables, her bucket full, face beaming.

But then, she was a gardener in the grand tradition of English gardeners, so I now forgive her. And I have come to understand her a little better.

With my new-found love of gardening, I understand the joy of pottering around on a quiet weekend, of the solitude and involvement. I understand why I can barely recall seeing her inside her cottage on a hillside, staring out over the intricacies of green countryside to the Black Mountains guarding the Welsh border, and why she was always out terracing, planting, creating stone paths and rockeries, and shrubberies through which we galloped on imaginary ponies – my sister's always white, mine always a piebald. Gardeners are, perhaps, poets with a more practical bent.

Why the English have a strong tradition of gardeners and garden designers is anyone's guess. Perhaps it was part of their conceit to take an area, shape, mould, control it and make it theirs. Perhaps it is a reflection of the more intimate nature of the English countryside.

But now, strangely, I find some of it in me. I find an innate eye for planning and design, and a complete satisfaction in creating an environment I'm content in.

§   §   §   §   §

I have now given the house a name – the house with the English cottage garden face it presents to the world, and the Australian bush hidden inside the gates. Munjon – a mostly forgotten word used for an Aboriginal person brought up in white society. Presenting one face, another colour to its soul.

Naming the house seemed the right thing to do, in keeping with its era and its rebirthing.

The important homes of my childhood seemed like living members of the family. They had character and personality. They had dogs and people, noise and silence, and the smell of cooking. And they had names.

Bruce Chatwin

I FIRST MET BRUCE CHATWIN IN 1977. It happened in a quiet bookshop in England. I was trawling the shelves and suddenly Bruce was there in front of me. A shock of blond hair, somewhat childish clothes. He looked very English. Then, he looked a little like me.

His first work, In Patagonia, was newly published and I was interested in the strange stories of that part of South America. I was interested in the genre of travelling writers. And I was interested in Bruce. He was everything I thought I wanted to be. So it was not surprising that we should connect so strongly.

There was also the fact that we both came from quite English backgrounds and shared a sense of "looking" – both at the physical world and for something less immediate or obvious. Something, perhaps, in ourselves.

The voice in Bruce's book sounded, to me, rather like mine. And his mind worked in a way that seemed so close to my own way of thinking that, at times, it verged on the unnerving. Bruce Chatwin instantly became a friend. A close friend – someone I felt I really knew. He became a pivotal (and enduring) part of my life, although I knew Bruce himself was much less needy.

I knew Bruce before the general public did. Before he became a Literary Force. Much less, and far worse, a Household Name.

I started travelling with Bruce, most notably through the more remote regions of the Australian continent. Through more complex places, geographic and personal. By then he had written The Songlines – a classic work of observation, thought and collection which was based in Australia and published in 1987. Sadly, it has become a sort of literary pop song.

Bruce had seen the Outback through his own eyes, and understood some parts of it and mistaken others – or, at least, interpreted it so strongly that its colours changed, showing him to be as human as me, or you. Unlike the popular idiom, he had not left only footprints. He had left a real mark.

Whenever I set off on a new journey – physical and metaphysical – I always made sure Bruce came along. In fact, he never missed a trip. I would find myself in long, if wordless, conversations with this man who had become a mentor to me. He was showing me the way not only to vision and understanding, but to finding my own literary voice.

Around the world, you will find thousands of people who literally met Bruce Chatwin. Perhaps he stayed with them throughout his travels and writing. Hundreds have boasted that "he wrote (this-or-that book) at my house". Although we never came face to face in the flesh, and although I only ever took him on my journeys in the form of a now-battered hardback first edition of The Songlines, I feel I have spent more intimate time with Bruce than any of them. Our relationship has endured more than two decades and the constant revelations about Bruce that make him not what I thought, or what I understood at the time. Things that could turn you away from a person, but have not.

I was quite prepared to believe that Bruce was dying from some extremely rare viral disease he had contracted in a little known valley in inner China. (I think that was how he reportedly explained it). When, on his deathbed, he was interviewed about his entry into the Booker Prize, I was horrified by a glimpse of him in hospital, skeletal. I was even more horrified when another author took a callous swipe at "Bruce's AIDS" and instantly scooped that author's books from my shelves, took them outside and consigned them to the dustbin. From that moment he has not been welcome in my house.

I was equally defensive of my old friend when his long-time editor, Susannah Clapp, published the book With Chatwin, describing his various character traits and foibles in excruciating detail. It seems to me that the relationship between writer and editor is based on trust (most writers – and certainly Bruce – being largely insecure about their work). In exposing their most intimate discussions and Bruce's private thoughts and shared fears, it seems to me that trust was broken.

But I had read it (which I suppose makes me, indefensibly, an accessory), as I had, unwittingly, absorbed other dubious rumours and truthful insights into Bruce's character. It was the character of a man I had not known. Gradually, two Bruce Chatwins have been taking shape. There was the Bruce I met in 1977, the young man in Jerry Bauer's famous – definitive – black and white photographic portrait, which has appeared on many of his book jackets. Sitting casually in shirt and jeans on the floor, back to a wall – with an intensity in his gaze which fixes you solidly. The Bruce Chatwin through whose eyes I looked when his photographs were published after his death, and whose vision and photographic "angles" I recognised and understood – recognised clearly enough to make me nod quietly. Yes, at this moment I can see through his eyes, and his vision is just what I had understood through his words.

Then there was the noisy, never-stop-talking, take-take-take Chatwin. The Birmingham boy who didn't gain a Degree, who invented and reinvented himself, whom Nicholas Shakespeare paints in the greatest detail in his 600-page, door-stopper of a biography "Bruce Chatwin". At the front are four solid pages of type, filled with a list of names of people Shakespeare approached for recollections as he stalked Chatwin for eight years. Chatwin's family, friends, acquaintances, classmates, house cleaners, artists, scientists, photographers, publishers, girlfriends, boyfriends. You name it. Writers from Salman Rushdie to Les Murray. More than 450 names from all over the world.

Shakespeare traces every step of Chatwin's life through these people, and throws in conclusions based on his years of study and interviews. "Chatwin was a storyteller, first, but not until the last third of his life did he write the stories down," he tells us. Salman Rushdie adds: "He was looking for stories the world could give him and that he could embellish. He didn't give a damn whether they were true or not; only whether they were good."

Shakespeare paints a picture of a colourful, frenetic character. The sort of person you can't quite work out. A man who married Elizabeth in 1965, and whose strange marriage endured 23 years, although he was a practicing homosexual. Of whom she said: "I always knew he was ambidextrous." ("I sometimes think he wasn't a person; he was a scrum," says the art critic, Robert Hughes.) A man with "a crowded address book where Jackie Onassis is listed next to an Oryx herder."

A man who, in the words of art historian Hugh Honour had a mind "filled with an extraordinary jumble of the abstruse, the exotic, the savage and the sophisticated". A man of whom German film director Werner Herzog says: "It's the resonance of the voice and the depth of the vision that makes him one of the truly great writers of our time."

Shakespeare's book skilfully follows Chatwin's life, from his schooldays to his early and very successful days in the art world at Sotheby's auctioneers, to his travels, through his writing to his illness and death from AIDS in 1989 (an illness he described as "my inexplicable fever").

He paints a picture of an extraordinarily gifted person who would not consider anything so menial as helping with washing up – who never would have thought of it. Who was said to have burst into a bathroom while one hostess was in the bath, to sit on the toilet and relieve himself, all the while chattering away. Who would invite guests to his home and then quickly tire of them and abandon them at a neighbour's house. Or abandon them in his home, come to that, declaring the urgent need to go and write. Who reportedly was equally happy, and eager, to have sex with either male or female, but only ever once.

I didn't know this Bruce Chatwin.

So, perhaps the man I knew wasn't even Bruce Chatwin at all. Perhaps it was just a mentor and icon I created (the portrait photograph fitted this figure perfectly). Perhaps it was idealised. Perhaps it was an alter ego. I have been considering that, in effect, I made Bruce Chatwin up.

If that is the case, I think it is fine. And certainly it is generally easier with writers like Chatwin than with, say, footballers, movie stars or rock singers, about whom we know too much. Or think we do.

The singer-songwriter and bass player Sting seems to understand this contract. At the end of an interview in the mid-90s, he was asked what he thought of the way the mass media had treated him. He smiled, the corners of his mouth turning upwards. He said he read about this character Sting in the popular press, and all the things this character Sting had done. They were things he had not done himself.

Character Sting was, he said, a person he didn't know – but

read about just like all the other readers did. The media had created a character they needed for a readership which needed it.

As a storyteller himself, he seemed to accept this.

I received an invitation to meet Sting once, but turned it down.

It is often a mistake to meet your heroes, or people whose work you particularly admire or seem to personally connect with. I've learned this over the years. At worst they aren't at all what you thought, at best they are mere humans, or not terribly engaging, or totally uninterested in you.

At first glance it might seem quite irrational that this feels unfair and an imbalance in a relationship they have no knowledge of and didn't ask for. Or did they? Didn't they, in fact, start it? Wasn't it they who approached the general public as an audience for their ideas and talents? Wasn't it they who hoped to touch individuals and make them disciples of their specific voice? It seems to me it was. They started the relationship.

I recently turned down an invitation to meet Henry Rollins. On another occasion I was scheduled to have lunch with Robyn Davidson in Sydney (I met her in her book Tracks, and fell unquestionably in love with her) but rang her agent at the last minute to cancel having fallen literally, but conveniently, ill.

And if I'd met Bruce Chatwin? Would we have been mates? I don't want to think about it. There are few things more depressing than feeling you have been deceived, or deceived yourself, about a person. With increasing revelations about Bruce Chatwin, for a time I felt I had been a fool all these years. Bruce wasn't Bruce after all. Not at all.

And then I got the books out (which I keep together on a special shelf) and scattered them across the loungeroom floor. I picked up On the Black Hill, the story of Welsh brothers Lewis and Benjamin Jones (for 42 years, sleeping side by side in their parents' bed, at the farm which was known as The Vision), published in 1982.

Utz, the story of the Meissen porcelains, published in 1988. And so on.

In each, the language is as I have always known it, their populations unchanged. The colours and atmosphere are the same. I can breath the air, and even the smells are as they were. More importantly, the voice is the same, and the presence behind them is steady. Bruce is there, alright, and it is the Bruce I have known for more than two decades. The Bruce I met in a quiet English bookshop in 1977.

Indeed, it is I who have changed enormously. I feel like quite a different person and, now living on the west coast of Australia, couldn't be in a more different place.

Shortly after finishing Nicholas Shakespeare's book I read an article he had written about the work:

> A biography prompts multiple unravellings. The biographer cannot revisit the past on his own, but requires the help of his subject's family, friends and enemies to unravel their past as well.

> In my grandmother's dining room in Malvern (in Worcestershire), overlooking the Welsh mountains, Hugh Chatwin (Bruce's brother) takes the scalpel one last time to the trickiest chapter of his brother's biography, an account of their early years in Birmingham after the war. Creaky at first, his memory now has the dexterity of someone who has reclaimed their childhood.

My own memory creaks and reclaims part of my own childhood. It hears my mother's accounts of her early years in Birmingham after the war, as we sat in her dining room in Malvern, overlooking the Welsh mountains. My first, childish hand-made books strewn over the floor.

The two Bruce Chatwins may be separate or one, illusionary or factual, but they are both part of my history and future.

Public Swimming Baths

NO DUCKING
NO BOMBING
NO PETTING

THE OLD PUBLIC SWIMMING BATHS was a deep, turquoise rectangle lined with flaking concrete. The water was always icy – the only way in was to brace yourself, stand on the edge, toes over the lip, count down (make yourself promise to dive on zero), and force yourself. I remember once counting from 20: 19, 18, 17, then resorting to mathematical fractions when I got to two ... "one and seven-eighths ... one and six-eighths ..."

When you did hit the water, the physiological and psychological impact was explosive.

There was the noise – the muffled, tin-can sound of the world above, the vibrating, whale-song echoes of the excitement and hard work below and, above all, the chorus of bubbles, bursting from your body and screaming past your ears. The bubbles seemed to have sound in them, only barely audible, but which deepened in tone with the length of the dive.

And there was the cold – leaching heat directly from your brain, ripping along your thin, white ribs, stripping the flesh from your thighs. It was like diving through staggered rows of tiny, white, razor-sharp teeth. Like dodging piranhas.

Then you would burst back out into the sunshine with a huge gasp and scream, and thrash immediately off in a fast crawl. Activity equalled warmth.

The lifeguard sat in a high-chair, like a tennis referee, watching, chatting up the girls (too white, too lumpy, with rolls of puppy fat, and strangely square-bottomed 70s bikinis), and wearing a shiny, stainless steel whistle – the complete armoury, with which he ruled.

NO DUCKING   NO BOMBING   NO PETTING

I committed none of the misdemeanours outlined on the warning sign. I thrashed a few too-cold "widths", avoided the big boys who were trouble-making and sat on the cracked concrete surrounds to warm my skinny, almost-transparent body.

From my favourite sitting spot, you could see the intricately designed Winter Gardens (a quaint and intriguingly old-fashioned name and concept, even then). The pond, the ducks, the prettily arched walking bridges, immaculate lawns and colourful borders. The flimsy flowers in patterns, perhaps with a clockface, perhaps spelling a word.

I sat amid the childish shrieks and contemplated the astonishing range of hills which were their backdrop, my spiritual rock and the home and inspiration of Sir George Bernard Shaw and Sir Edward Elgar, who I already understood to have been England's finest composer and a violinist like myself, though rather better.

I can't now remember going to the swimming baths with friends, though I suspect I must have. It seems to me it was always a solitary business, one of observation and reflection as much as participation.

There were two diving boards and a springboard. The springboard was achievable, though I once saw a boy try a twisting dive, dosed with far more testosterone than is healthy, and watched by too big an audience of girls willing to be impressed. He split his chin open as the board recoiled and whacked him. It cut in slow motion, spraying red blood droplets against a china blue sky, where they hung stationary for a moment that seemed long. He tumbled messily, like a thrown toy, into the water, leaking a scarlet stain. The lifeguard lept down his ladder and dived, flat and fast, to retrieve the body. It looked dead on the concrete, until it convulsed blood and snot in an arcing spray over the thrilled, clamouring bodies that had surrounded it.

The springboard had a strange wheel contraption which could be moved further down its length, changing the amount of spring. Girls didn't move it. Boys, it seemed to me, moved it a distance commensurate with the number of girls watching.

The lower diving board was also something I felt to be achievable, but which I should save for later years. I imagined that if you closed your eyes, held your nose, landed flats-of-feet first and waited patiently to rise again to the surface, as the laws of nature surely decreed you must, no real harm could possibly come to you.

But holding your nose was a problem. The brave boys didn't. They raced the board and howled off the lip, describing any number of wildly elaborate shapes on the way down, before hitting the surface in deliberate disorder to create an awesome splash. The performance was rated by the loudness of the cheers.

The thought of quietly walking the plank and plopping undramatically into the water whilst delicately pinching my nostrils was not to be contemplated at this stage.

The high board, on the other hand, was not to be contemplated at any stage. It was an impossible feat, although I had repeatedly seen people (even girls) do it, looking straight ahead, with the nonchalant assurance of one crossing a busy highway protected only by the flimsy plastic circle of a pedestrian light. Wearing the same distant, glazed expression.

After the swim I would paddle back through the muddy dressing room and twang the numbered rubber band off my ankle. (I wore it there as my wrist was too small and I feared losing it. Such a loss was the stuff of nightmares. It could separate me from my clothes forever and force me to walk the many kilometres home in my bathers.) I would hand the band to the big man or bored girl behind the Formica counter and they would vanish for a minute and then return to slide me a basket containing my clothes and my "valuables" in one shoe. Such relief.

I hated changing. I have never been good at drying and still contort a wet body into dry clothes, which cling and fit skewwhiffly. But there was always a reward. Hot chocolate in a plastic cup after an ice-cold swim seemed to me one of the greatest imagineable pleasures. Too hot, too sweet and too delicious.

That was all 30 years ago.

The Winter Gardens are still there, still the same. And the Winter Gardens halls where, as a child, I heard so many classical concerts and which, in its formal oblongness, so resembled a railway station, has been changed inside into a racy new "artspace", though the facia remains the same.

And the Public Swimming Baths has gone completely.

In its place, just past the duck pond, under the high green walls of the Malvern Hills, is The Splash – a modern cathedral which, an official there tells me, definitely takes the THE. (I call it "Splash" but am corrected. It is "THE Splash".)

For a start, the pool is now indoors, allowing heating and all-year use. (In a way this seems a shame: I have always enjoyed the sight of an empty swimming pool, its bottom leaf-tattoed. It seems to me one of our few tangible remaining connections with the seasons.)

The Splash is not really a swimming pool. It is an Entertainment. Warm as a bath, kidney bowl shaped, the tiled beach lapped by waves every hour.

Before the wave machine is started, the lifeguards – all rather too young to be taken seriously, but still in regulation red and yellow – are galvanised by a frenzy of instruction and concern. Their chorus of whistles orders out all the floating objects which have previously been put in (seemingly in an allotted time slot) for us to play with, which we dutifully do.

It begins slowly. The first three or four surges pass almost unnoticed, then the whole body of water seems to draw in and out. Lifting and pulling us, now crammed in the water shoulder to shoulder. Dragging the smallest children up and down the tiled beach, and the mass of swimmers up and down the pool. I hang around the far edge, in a metre and a half of water, where it seems most dangerous.

Quickly it is over, and quickly it is calm.

Then there is the slide – a long, twisting snake hanging from the ceiling, flushed by water, reached by a high spiral staircase. The warmth up under the roof makes waiting your turn pleasurable. From up here, you can watch the heads bobbing, the children playing. A moving, flowing, noisy tableau.

Then I am sitting at the top of the slide watching the round disc of a red light. The red goes off and the green comes on. I pull hard on the stainless steel handrails, lie flat, try to get some speed up for the first turn. Press on my right heel and left shoulder and lift the weight off my body, just like my brother told me. "Reduces friction, increases speed." On the second turn, I go high up the wall – this is warm luge, in water not ice.

It flattens out and I walk out of the final dip, self-conscious at my child-like pleasure.

Then return to the too-warm soup of chlorine, snot, urine, dead skin and floating sticking plasters. A chemical soup I am too scared to put my head under – a soup of imagined organisms.

Whistles sound and it is time once again to play with floating toys, or to sit on the plastic chairs under beach umbrellas, by big glass windows framing the hills. This view is somehow incongruous above the painted scene of a tropical beach which runs around the walls.

Or time, perhaps, to sit in the cafe (to the sound of video games), or go to the gym, or "tan to peach" on the row of sunbeds.

Interestingly – strangely, it strikes me – The Splash is not about sex. Despite all that warmth, all that flesh, the languid nature of the place, the virtual nudity, there's no underlying urge in the air. But then, this morning is more about families than teenagers, so it would appear the urges have been largely spent.

The conversion of the Public Swimming Baths to The Splash is, perhaps, symptomatic of the change from the remembered to the present. Symptomatic of our modern need to be entertained.

The Splash is a steamy, sticky womb of a place, not a confronting cold pit. It is a symbol of our softness and desire for comfort and pleasure and instruction. And of the loss of simplicity and spirit.

Green Card

THE GREEN CARD WAS DIVIDED into three parts (each folding into the other) and five of the six sides were covered with small boxes. To a nervous nine-year-old, this seemed an insurmountable number of boxes, particularly as each required a weekly cross and each cross required two shillings.

Two shillings was the sort of Big Money my mother walked a round trip of several kilometres carrying heavy shopping bags to save, rather than taking the bus into town. It was enough to put food on the table. And so it was that each Monday morning, when I handed over a two shilling coin, it was done with a mixture of guilt and amazement.

With every cross, the green card became more dog-eared, and the violin became more mine.

The green card represented an impossible passage of time and an investment, in every sense, that should have been beyond a child's comprehension. But, in fact, I did completely comprehend it. I look back at that small boy and wonder at what he knew, and how he knew so much, and how he could have forgotten it. It seems to me he was old beyond his years, and sensitive to the point of pain.

At the time my mother was routinely finding two shillings from the corner of her purse on a Monday morning (and dinner money and everything else for me, my older sister and younger brother), she was having a hard time. I knew she was worried about money, and I did everything I could (if only in terms of moral support) to bear some of that weight.

One week she had a big house and a daily help to clean it, and the next she was on her knees in another town, scrubbing floors and trying to make ends meet. Coping with three children, very little money and the fallout from her dead marriage. And trying to give us every opportunity.

My violin teacher was a man called Percy Smith. Mr Smith was the lead First Violinist in the local orchestra, which to me was the greatest orchestra in the world, and a gathering of the finest musicians. Of them all, Mr Smith (white-fingered, dressed in tweeds, always lightly scented) was the finest, and playing the finest instrument.

I had no doubt then (and I have a sneaking suspicion that I still feel it) that orchestras are only designed ... were only invented ... to surround and support violins. The violin is as close to perfect design as I can imagine. It is an extension of the human voice, in the broadest sense. It is a neat, individual, living amplifier for human emotion.

And my violin was among them.

Thirty years later, the violin is still one of my most prized possessions, which are few and almost all musical instruments. I recently told a fine violin maker how my mother had struggled to buy the instrument for me, and he was good hearted enough to say that, although a Chinese factory instrument, it had a good sound.

I cannot judge this. I have listened to thousands of violins throughout my life. Shared a room with some of the best in the world ... instruments that literally vibrated the walls and the cavity within my chest ... and I cannot judge my own. It is too loaded with memory and emotion.

It is the right colour – not too red in the finish – with only honourable marks from its years of use. It lives in a well-kept black case with green felt lining and is wrapped in a silk scarf which was my mother's. I have only one bow, though there are mounts for two.

In the little "secret compartment" at the head of the case are various remainders of the knobs of resin used to dust the bow. Some are round, some just the sliver remnants of rectangular pieces. Only one piece is of any use for treating the bow's horse hair, but the others are its diary.

Under the neck of the violin, a shoulder rest is stowed. It is a simple metal rest, covered in black velvet, which clips onto the violin and then rests on the shoulder to help support the violin in its right attitude. I have seen many types over the years – revolutionary designs! – but I see in the local music store that this style is again being manufactured, now in plastic.

Mr Smith gave me this shoulder rest. It was his own, and when he bought a new one of the same design, he gave me his. It is a prized possession. Mr Smith had hundreds of students, I imagine, but he gave the shoulder rest to me. And now that I look at it, three decades later, I realise that it is unmarked. The black velvet is undamaged. Even the tiny rubber covers on each of the feet are all still in place.

It seems to me there can only have been one reason why he replaced it.

In return for Mr Smith's confidence in me, I played every day. I relished scales and arpeggios and waded through simple childish tunes that seemed quite infantile. Then we moved into baroque music and my mind changed and my life changed.

An American academic recently published findings of research which showed that playing a keyboard for 15 minutes a day will increase a child's spatial IQ by 46 per cent. (Spatial intelligence allows us to perceive and understand the visual world accurately. It helps us to form mental images.)

Dr Frances Rauscher, assistant professor of psychology at the University of Winsconsin, monitored pre-school children learning music and others who were not. After eight months, her research showed that the spatial reasoning performance of the musical group far exceeded the others.

In particular, a musical education may help a child to learn mathematics and science, Dr Rauscher was reported as saying.

Dr Rauscher then conducted a second experiment, working with college students. After listening to a Mozart piano sonata for two hours, the students' spatial IQ was immediately higher than those who had been kept in a silent room, or given relaxation instructions.

A recent documentary on the brain explained this further. We are born with twice the number of neurons that we require. In early years, electrical pathways are opened, networks built, a lace-work of activity established, which always remain in place even if not in continual use. Music is particularly effective at doing this. The documentary confirmed that that doesn't necessarily mean you will be a great musician. Those networks and pathways may be used for other processes – Mozart may improve your arithmatic.

I can't vouch for the scientific validity of these ideas. But, combined, they make a lot of sense to me, and are broadly borne out by a recent experience.

I played voilin for many years, then just stopped. I wrapped the instrument in its silky shroud, laid it in its felt-lined coffin and just walked away – not from the violin itself, which I love as much as the day the first cross was applied to the green card – but from making the sound. I told people I felt I had settled on a plateau and could go no further. I now suspect that there were two factors at work (and the Plateau Theory had nothing to do with either).

I have always been interested by why musicians chose their instruments, particularly children starting out. What comes into that choice of bassoon or flute or bass or French horn or electric bass guitar or piano? Or violin, for that matter. Circumstance, sure – but it is very much to do with the sound in our head, the sound we instinctively want to make.

For some reason (and I suspect the second factor was a leaving behind of the past) I didn't want to make that sound any more. It was the sound of the first half of my life. And I had a new sound in my head and wanted to start a new life.

So, as an adult, I took up guitar. First some years of classical training on a nylon-string guitar. Classical guitar has relatively little music written specifically for it, and much of that is early Mediterranean. Guilani et al.

I struggled with triplets and vaguely Spanish sounds. Then a piece of baroque music came into the proceedings. A piece I had never seen or heard before. Yet I recognised its form. My mind instinctively worked that way.

I have no doubt that my brain was instinctively working in networks and pathways that had been established 30 years earlier. They were still there, and they understood this structure.

"You should start young."

There is a commonly held belief that children learn an instrument more easily, and better, than adults can. Perhaps elements of this are true. (Certainly they can be physically and maybe mentally more flexible.)

But, speaking from personal experience, I have learnt faster and more thoroughly as an adult. Ah, but an adult who has a musical background as a child, you may say. I argue that this makes learning a new instrument more difficult, as there are technical things to be unlearnt, and instinctive things to be trained out of yourself through practice. You must learn to read the music differently.

But greater maturity has its advantages. I am learning because I want to learn. I am learning for my own pleasure and meditation. Certainly not for competition or exams. In a game of plateaux, if I struggle with a technique or particular piece of music, I have the patience to plug away at it, comfortable in the knowledge that eventually I will get it. I view it as a long-term project, and one with no objective other than to enjoy it in the present. I know that in five, then 10 years, reward and repertoire will be greater.

As a 10-year-old voilinist, I won a bust of Beethoven (my hero composer at that time) for having the most musical promise in the school. I was disappointed that it was plastic not plaster, but it was presented as, and represented, a real possibility of a career in music. I keep it next to the violin.

§   §   §   §   §

Some time after I told the violin maker the story of how my instrument was earnt and paid for, he said he wanted to restore it – for the instrument itself, and for what it represents.

The Luthier

SCOTT WISE'S FINGERS ARE BLUNT, dark and calloused. The nails are cracked and somehow curly, and some of them have broken away. Generally, the hands' creases, and the tiny troughs of scars, folds and fingerprints are filled black, ingrained. On this day, a couple of the knuckles are also damaged, and there are small nicks and cuts. The nails have neither the obsessively smooth finish of a classical guitarist, nor are they those expected of fine artist. These are knockabout, hard yakka sort of hands.

And yet they can do remarkable and delicate things. Watching them rub together, awaiting the arrival of dinner, I can't help think it's rather like using a chainsaw for keyhole surgery.

Scott Wise, luthier and musician, is in good form. He has come up from his home near the legendary Aussie surf of Margaret River to perform with The Ten Cent Shooters at a Perth music festival in the landlocked suburb of Midland. Even though Scott's a mate, and I like the Shooters' bluesy music, I didn't go to watch. Near the coast, it was hot enough to peel the tread from your tyres, and I just couldn't face all the pulsating paved surfaces in Midland.

Scott confirms it was hot. Bloody hot. "And how was the gig?" They played well, he says, with that certain Wise, analytical honesty (this question is usually met with an answer somewhere between "good" and "terrible"). But not many people turned up, he adds, pink-eyeing me.

I should explain those pink eyes. They are the familiar blood-shot eyes of surfers. Wise dumped his city roots for the Margaret River surf some years ago and early most mornings you'll find him out in the swell somewhere, waiting for a set. Contemplating as much as surfing. Then he goes home to a house buzzing with family getting ready for school. Then he heads out to his shed.

This shed is, in fact, the workshop where Scott Wise, luthier, creates fine musical instruments. It is where the 200 instruments he has built over more than 20 years, and the 6000 he has handled, repairing and restoring, also have their voice through the next guitar, voilin, dulcimer, electric bass . . . whatever happens to be on the bench.

There are two ways of looking at the shed.

You can either say it is a woodwork shop, where small amounts of exotic timbers are cut, shaped, bent to fit a very specific pattern. Glued, fixed, finished, strung, tested. Where a plan, a design, a blue-print, is followed with the greatest attention to detail. Or you can see it as a laboratory, communication centre, philosophy depart-ment, birthing centre, nursery. In that order: that is the process.

I have already told you I am a friend of Scott's. Just because he's a good bloke – a nice mix of strong, sensitive and silly. It's not worth telling you how I met him, but I will tell you how I really got to know him. It was through a particular instrument – through a sound in my head, which I managed to communicate to him, which he managed to piece together in his, through both listening to me and knowing me. A sound which he heard, then built an acoustic guitar to make. Rolling thunder in the bass, harpsichord-fine at the top end. At the first stroke, it made the sound that had been in my head. It was the most remarkable moment – a realisation of the potential and rewards of true and complete communication.

That might sound a bit over the top, but not if you accept that a handmade musical instrument is more than a sum of its parts, more than a timber sound box with strings. Not if you accept that it takes life from the hand that shaped it.

Historic Italian violins have been completely analysed by computers – every width and density measured, the glue ingredients established, the varnish reconstructed by high-tech techniques. And when new instruments have been constructed mechanically to these precise criteria, they have sounded, well, ordinary. Something happens when an instrument is made by hand. It is something to do with human spirit. I can only tell you that I know this for sure, because I have heard it and felt it under my fingers, and so have generation upon generation of real musicians.

I am with Scott Wise when a shipment of rare timbers arrives from India. He has imported 450 sets of "blanks" ... necks, sides, backs, all handstitched into neat hessian bundles.

He selects the 30 sets he will keep – "the trouble of importing them gives me the choice of materials and funds those materials for me" – not by appearance, but by ear. He painstakingly holds "backs" to his ear and taps each, looking for a certain Ring. Looking for the Wise Sound. Reluctantly discarding the visually spectacular if it sounds "dead" to his ear (these are onsold for factory guitars).

"Three amazing things have happened to me this year," says Scott.

One was a "jam session" at a guitar camp in the United States of America, where the music, and somehow the fellowship of the musicians, took off, left the Earth, whirled around in the ether and eventually ... only eventually ... came back down. It just got caught up in its own momentum.

Another was a similar, but not as intense, sensation at Bridgetown Blues Festival, in Western Australia.

In the third, though, Scott Wise says he felt like a wood molecule. For weeks he had been in the workshop 12 to 15 hours a day, totally focused on making a number of instruments. Working on the mathematical, technical, spiritual, creative conundrum that defines each. Totally concentrating. Totally absorbed. Until he could FEEL how the pieces would vibrate, how the glues would hold them, how scraping them thinner and thinner with a simple curve of metal would affect the sound. He could feel it in an intrinsic, instinctive, organic way.

Some months earlier he had told me how he had recently come to fully understand that the most important thing was to be able to "hear" an instrument before he started making it. If he could hear it clearly, every choice he made would lead to that sound. He would select the right pieces of timber, cut them right, thin them right, build them to that sound. Conscious decisions, yet somehow they become part of a subconscious process.

This would make sense to Scott Wise, whose life has been, and still is, shaped by both. The conscious and subconscious. What is on the surface and what is below the surface.

On the surface, Wise is the son of former Western Australian Labor Premier Frank (Scott) Wise, and grandson of a Mayor of Coolgardie, who invented the Coolgardie Safe – a contraption used in the Goldrush interior of Australia, where dampened hessian kept food inside cool and fresh.

Walking across damp beach sand, on a classic Cottesloe early morning (not far from where he went to primary school), Scott remembers how he used to hang around there as a kid in the 60s.

He and his mates would sift the sand with tennis racquets, looking for coins. Then he joined the surf club, and ran the soft sand to North Cottesloe and the hard sand back before "swimming about a bit".

He learnt to swim from an old hand, who had him doing laps of doggy paddle, learning how to pull himself through the water. He shows me. He actually seems to pull himself over the water, like a kid crawling along, playing soldiers. He leaves a bow wave behind him. That's how the old timer had learnt too "and he'd only take one stroke for everyone else's five," as Scott remembers it. "He taught me to swim efficiently. Not fast, but efficient."

This morning we just swim over to the groyne, stopping on the way. He sits in the water, the surfer. I loll around on my back, staring at toes and horizon. "The ocean's so DIFFERENT here," says Scott. And in this he seems to gauge not just the difference between the soft, flat Indian Ocean protected behind Cottesloe's rocky wall and that raw Margaret River swell, but between the young turk who used to race in the sand and this now mature man.

The ocean, his age, and his 20th anniversary of instrument making have conflagrated into a moment for reflection. Somehow this morning, and the previous night's motorcycle "laps" round the slick cafe strips – just a couple of kids on a night out – and Scott's disappointment that the older lady bathers at Cottesloe wear all sorts of swimming caps now (not just white) are part of a revisiting. I feel we have stood together at a gateway between past and future.

Consciously, that young Cottesloe primary school kid's future was to go to Swanbourne High, before chosing a career in geology, and achieving his degree at the University of Western Australia.

Subconsciously, there was always music in him.

He broke away and turned to that music, playing in a string of venues and bands. Then came the Fremantle Shop days. Wise opened for business in Quarry Street, making his bread and butter repairing instruments but starting to make them too.

I've seen a couple of early instruments and they are not as fine as today's. You wouldn't expect them to be. His art has been, and will continue to be, refined with both experience in the craft and his own maturity.

Today his instruments are keenly sought by enthusiasts aware of the standards of international excellence. These are people who could afford a handmade instrument from Spain, Ireland, Canada, the US, but choose Scott's. People are prepared to wait for their masterpiece. Their piece of individuality. Their heirloom. Wise has enough orders to keep busy for two years. Enough orders to feel pressured by the workload.

He is where he has always wanted to be – making his living from playing music and making new instruments, living near the surf. He doesn't have to rely on repair work to pay the bills. And there are constant gigs for Scott and his wife Louisa Wise, and The Ten Cent Shooters. Louisa is a champion American fiddler, and their performances and CD recordings are popular.

That recording, and technical sound computer work for many other artists, is done at their Margaret River home by Scott. When he's not in the shed or making music, he's fiddling round with it, technically speaking, on computer.

When I was talking with another Australian band, they mentioned that Scott mastered their CD. Visiting a recording studio in the north of Australia, I find a black Scott Wise electric bass on a stand, and one of the local Pigram Brothers band playing a Wise mandolin. They'd known him for years, they said. And Scott tells me their dad, Eric, had inspired his instrument making. Eric used to make instruments for his kids in the back shed out of pretty well anything he could lay his hands on. They still play them too – alongside Scott's.

After Scott visited him and saw this, as an enthusiastic but all-but-broke youth, he came back to Perth and spent the money he had on timbers to send to Eric. He has since passed on the encouragement and enthusiasm by teaching instrument making in Denmark, Western Australia. (He recently took an order for a guitar from the other Denmark, in Europe.)

Among the handfuls of snapshots that Louisa keeps in a box, there are a number of Scott in the forest, cutting naturally fallen logs. He is sensitive about the precious nature of the timber he uses and, in that sense, a custodian of their environment.

These unusual woods give unique qualities and, obviously, his musicians want unique instruments. Scott was recently asked to build an acoustic guitar for a man who wanted it to be strong enough to chuck in the back of his ute without a case, with strings that wouldn't rust, and which would be "square" enough to stand vertically on its end, unaided (I can't imagine why). Scott Wise built it out of Western Australian wandoo. And it sounded good.

Another enthusiast brings drawings and recordings of South American instruments, his passion. Wise researches and then makes them, to add to the private collection.

§   §   §   §   §

It was Louisa's idea to mark Scott's 20th anniversary with two special concerts. Owners of Scott Wise instruments turned up to play them ... professionals alongside those who had never played in public before ... farmers singing original songs ... folk players, classical ... humourous, romantic ... concerts which seemed to capture not only the very essence of music, but the strength of bond between musicians. The Ten Cent Shooters on stage, with Scott Wise playing mandolin, harmonica and singing.

Shortly before the biggest, second concert, I rang Scott's sister Rose, who was stage managing the evening (and playing a classical piece with Louisa). Rose sounded just a little harassed. "It must be a nightmare," I offer. "It's not like there are just a couple of professional bands to organise."

"Yes," she says. "Scott just said there would be '40 to 50'. I said, 'what, acts or individuals?' He just said 'oh, about that. Yes, I think so'."

Sometimes you are not sure if Scott Wise is hearing you or not. The pink eyes are somewhat glazed. But then he can surprise you. He can, after a minute, come back with a most insightful comment, showing that not only was he hearing you, but he was listening too. A comment which takes the thought or line of conversation forward by a huge leap. Other times, he's just not listening. Then I think he may just be hearing some other sound in his head.

§ § § § §

Scott Wise was staying at my house the other night, after a big gig. He rolled up late in his old truck, which frequently ticks and bleeds on the road outside.

He was exhausted, so I offered to help him carry gear in from the truck. It has only a garden shed latch on its flimsy cover.

He was almost incoherent. "I'm too tired. It doesn't matter."

"But what's in there?"

"Just sound equipment, amplifiers. Half a dozen instruments."

"But what if someone steals them?"

"I'll make some more."

Rose

I WILL ALWAYS THINK OF ROSE as someone who saved my life. Almost literally. I was badly injured in a motorcycle accident and Rose, an occupational therapist, took me on and cared for me. She got me through the pain and injuries.

We met in a booth at a clinic. I was in a surgical collar, in excruciating pain, and someone had foolishly laid me down on my back. I was now unable to move, and the agony caused by the weight on my neck can't be described. I remember it, and screaming at anyone who came close enough to threaten to touch me.

Rose was passing the curtains, and heard the noise inside. She stuck her head in and asked what was going on, instantly took in the desperate scene, then threw everyone out. Even the memory reminds me of Christ throwing the Pharisees out of the Temple.

Then she cradled me and told me she would help. It's hard to describe this moment. But it was, perhaps, the only moment in my life when I have totally given myself over to someone and completely trusted them.

Slowly, gently, over a long period, she got me up, and laid her hands on me and very gently massaged away some of the pain. They were moments as close to a miracle as I ever expect to experience.

I saw Rose daily, then gradually less frequently, over the next year as I recovered. And though we gradually lost contact, barely a day has passed when I haven't thought of her. Especially as I climb onto my new motorcycle every morning.

So it's strange that when I did see her again,
I didn't recognise her ...

§   §   §   §   §

The bar is thick with smoke and the crowd is pushed against the little stage in one corner. Someone has broken a glass, and I'm standing in it, squashed against a window, waiting for Aussie singer Deborah Conway (who will eventually come out to draw a gasp when she throws her arms up for the first time, revealing a massively black birdsnest under each arm, the recoil drawing a faint smile from the singer).

To be honest, the only reason that I'm enduring it all is to be this close to Deborah. And the only reason I'm enduring it all so long before she comes on is because I want a good spot. I claim it before the support act come on, though I generally don't like support acts.

The crowd obviously knows the two girls now playing in front of me. They have written the songs, both play guitars, sing with sharp, powerful voices.

The face of one haunts me. I feel I know her. Recognise her from somewhere. You know, the sort of experience when you know someone, but don't. Can't quite place the face or the context from which you know them.

The girl is dark, confident and, well, "Rocky". She's kind of confident and sexy. She looks like she could handle this bear-pit of a crowd easily enough if it turned nasty.

Suddenly I feel she looks a bit like Rose, someone I used to know. But Rose was, well, a goody-two-shoes, really. A straight-fringed, perfectly groomed, daintily spoken, part-time gospel singer.

The girl on stage looks like an alter-ego, parallel universe version of her. Like a cartooned Bad Rose.

After their act, after a bemused Conway has stepped onto the stage and mastered the Saturday Night crowd, I leave still puzzled.

Was that Rose?

§　　§　　§　　§　　§

"You should have come up after the show and said hello." I have just hugged Rose and she smells just the same, just as sweet as before. I'm embarrassed when I explain that I couldn't even work out if it was her. It was only when I checked out the names of the pair in the office library that I was sure.

But Rose shows no surprise when I try to explain this to her. The metamorphosis is an obvious one.

"I'm allowing myself to have fun," she explains simply, later. "I am allowing myself to be naughty." Allowing the person that was trapped inside her to come out. Being herself. Kids are naughty then learn to be good. If they are very lucky, they learn how to be naughty again, when they are adults.

Our friendship is re-established the moment we meet in the cafe. When the other half of the duet, arrives, I instantly like her too. All eyebrow ring and energy and enthusiasm, mixed with an exuberant and nicely acidic sense of humour.

§　　§　　§　　§　　§

The more time I spend with Rose, the more I realise that the person inside hasn't change much at all. The essence of Rose is still the same. Different but the same. She continues her work as an occupational therapist, but now from the home she shares with her singing partner, Martine. In a room that sits comfortably next to the Music Room (with its velvet-covered filing cabinets) she promotes physical and emotional wellness, and does deep tissue therapeutic and "maintenance" work.

"I want to facilitate wellness in my clinic," she explains. "And hope and wellness in my music.

"There's a very down to earth element to the job of healing, connecting one to one with people. Something very different to music." Different but the same.

§　　§　　§　　§　　§

Rose and Martine met at a gospel music festival in Sydney in 1993, and didn't really get on. "Martine thought I was aloof," says Rose. "That was in my glossy, glamour days."

But when Martine came to stay in Western Australia, they started working together and becoming friends. They wrote three songs in six days. When Martine went home to Sydney, they carried on writing together over the phone, running up $300 bills.

"There was a soul connection and a creative connection," says Rose. "A flurry of creativity. We couldn't stop it."

Martine moved to Perth and they started performing together. "It was scary as hell," says Martine, "just going into pubs, two girls." It was also scary as they were both soloists playing within a duet. "We had to work out the process of performing together," says Rose.

"I love the shades of dark and light that are between us as people, as performers, and in our hair. It's really important to us."

Through hundreds of shows over two years, they built a warm and supportive following. Soon they were performing 150 shows a year, and appearing on stage with The Black Sorrows, Tommy Emmanuel, Wedding Parties Anything, Ed Kuepper, The Waifs, James Reyne and international artists like Arlo and Abe Guthrie.

They have played a host of music festivals and released successful CDs. They found their way through to the airwaves of Australia, and even radio stations as far afield as Dublin, Massachusetts and Mexico.

The Velvet Janes (someone suggested Velvet Jones, Eddie Murphy's character in Saturday Night Live. "We feminised it," explains Rose) went on a successful five-week tour of California. Within three minutes of the first interval of the first show, they sold all the merchandise they had for the tour. At every concert, they received a standing ovation.

The Velvet Janes do things their own way. They worked hard, sang hard, saved their money and funded the American touring. They funded their first CD album, a collection of 13 original songs which cost $15,000 of their own, hard-earned money.

"We basically sing and play everything," says Martine.

Rose: "That's what our craft is. That's what we do."

Martine: "I have always wanted to develop my own style of guitar playing. Most of what I have learnt, I have learnt from books and tapes. I have never had lessons. I have adapted it to what I want to do."

Rose also learnt the hard way, making her musical debut aged eight at the Methodist Ladies Auxiliary, singing My Favourite Things, from The Sound of Music, which she learnt at the orphanage where she grew up. "Then I got sacked from church choirs for singing out of texture – too loud." While their gospel music days are behind them, and definitely not part of their shows or recordings, Rose adds: "The music is still inspired."

Martine: "Spiritually inspired."

Rose: "Music lifts my soul."

Well, Hallelujah.

§　　§　　§　　§　　§

Every time I hug Rose to say cheerio, I get a small electric shock. She has the same energy she had back in that booth when she was the other Rose. When you find friendship again, you shouldn't let it go.

Annie Leibovitz

THE SIGN ROLLING AROUND a building in Times Square says there are 46,694 minutes remaining to the start of the Atlanta Olympics. This could only be New York, where every second counts.

Particularly this morning.

Annie Leibovitz, who wears, a little uncomfortably, the tag of "the world's highest paid photographer", is working to finish an Olympic exhibition, with more than 120 images shot over two years.

She says the work is "very beautiful, very graphic, about line and form". She adds: "At a certain point it starts to bore the shit out of me."

In her unpretentious 11th floor studio at the edge of Manhattan Island, overlooking the docks and Hudson River, Annie

Leibovitz is being rather candid this morning. "I am not even sure if I am going to stay and do the Olympics because I feel like I have done it and I want to move on," she admits. "I am ready for something else."

So, do you have a short span of attention?

"No. I mean yes. Probably."

Mmmm.

A couple of years ago a friend sent her a page ripped from the New York Times which listed the 15 symptoms for Attention Deficit Disorder. "I got all 15! It's a disease I have! They have a name for this!"

Leibovitz is, as she will tell me when we meet again the next day, being "pretty straightforward" today. ("I shot from the hip there.") In fact, she's also just being funny. While she shares the reputation of most top photographers for being "difficult", Leibovitz's dry sense of humour should probably come as no surprise – if you look at the photographs that have made her arguably the most famous photographer in the world; in America, as famous as the big-ticket celebrities she shoots.

Whoopi Goldberg in a bath of milk. Clint Eastwood trussed up with rope on a dusty movie set. Roseanne and Tom Arnold mud wrestling. John Cleese hanging upside down from a tree, dressed like a bat. Tiny jockey Willie Shoemaker next to towering basketballer Wilt Chamberlain.

Even Demi Moore naked and pregnant on the cover of Vanity Fair had its share of humour – poking fun at American society's taboos. (The edition was eventually sold in America in a brown paper wrapper, amid a hullabaloo which attracted global attention.)

Then, to follow up, Demi Moore nude but with her body painted. The Blues Brothers painted blue. Artist Keith Haring painted black and white, with a long black line down his white penis (he was trying to make it look longer).

Ouch. Sore point.

It is "horrifying", she says, that the photograph isn't in the catalogue produced for the Japanese leg of the world tour of her work, which was a blitzing success through America, Europe and beyond.

"The catalogue is always very painful to look at. Censorship!" The voice is rising. "He's not naked to me." Now exasperated, and somewhat unnerving at full force. "It's a piece of art! Not a naked man." I am quick to agree that Haring seems to dissolve into the room in which he stands, which he had painted with a similar black and white pattern.

The exhibition of 171 works represents 13 years of work with Rolling Stone magazine and the past 12 with Vanity Fair – publications which she describes as "two luxury liners" and which have charted and defined US popular culture. Pictures which reflect her "pretty much American point of view".

Being attached to the magazines has given her access to a massive public and some of the most remarkable people and events of our time – from the early days of rock and roll to Richard Nixon's resignation to the final portrait of John Lennon, curled vulnerable and foetus-like beside Yoko Ono. A portrait taken just hours before he was killed.

The photographs were compiled in a book covering her work from 1970 to 1990, on which the exhibition is based, but updated with more recent pictures.

New photographs in bare, reportage style from Sarajevo, or black and white landscapes from Arizona, are far removed from the elaborate shoots for which she is most famous, and which see big crews "on set". Assistants, stylists, hairdressers, make-up artists, more assistants. Case upon case of gear.

"Sometimes I laugh when I turn round and see there are 20 people there taking the picture," she says. "It's like the old joke of how many people it takes to screw in a light bulb. You can get lost in the bigness of everything."

Leibovitz has just returned from the desert inland from Los

Angeles, where she had been shooting Sir Anthony Hopkins for Vanity Fair. It was, she admits, like a small movie set.

"I was thinking 'I have one of the greatest actors in the world in my Grade B photo essay here'. It was very funny. I was laughing."

But this shoot shows how she comes up with the ideas for her celebrity pictures. Her researcher had pulled together material on Sir Anthony. "In a couple of articles he said that the happiest time of his life was two weeks before he started shooting Silence of the Lambs, when he got in a car and drove across the US. He just loved the isolation of the car and driving.

"He likes being in cafes with sunglasses on and seeing if people recognise him. There is something seriously strange about that. Something beautiful and romantic. You can attach anything you want to it.

"As a photographer I immediately picked that up. It was obvious to me."

She talked to his agent, who said Sir Anthony had just driven back from Texas to Los Angeles – in a massively circuitous route via Seattle. So Leibovitz suggested they just go out into the desert and drive. "It was a great, great, great idea," she enthuses.

"We found a place in the desert which had a cafe, gas station and motel and we just took him out there and did driving shots and cafe shots. It was completely made up, but it was based on him. He just loved being out there and driving. He said 'this is exactly what I do'."

This is a subtle toning down of the bright, artificially lit, highly "styled" genre of picture which Leibovitz developed to help the newly-introduced colour photographs in Rolling Stone magazine reproduce well on its "rag paper".

The style was also a response to subjects having limited time – she couldn't just choose the best light conditions vital for colour photography, she had to create them. So she has developed a "vague formula", and asks for two or three days to do a portrait session.

It is an approach which is now widely copied.

"I see other people use it, but I don't feel ownership of it because it didn't come out of an emotional place," she says. "It came out of honesty about the fact that I wasn't there very long. I was trying to say 'this is a set up picture'.

"What disturbs me most is that there was a thought that I was asking people to jump into swimming pools for the sake of jumping into swimming pools for a photograph. That was disturbing to me because there is a great deal of thought in my photographs and the ideas really come from my subjects."

She pauses. "Even Sir Anthony Hopkins said he didn't want to do a 'jumping through flames' shot like I did for Tom Cruise and Mission Impossible." How could he think that, she wonders?

"I think it's because a lot of photographers abuse it. They ask people to do things that make no sense and are embarrassing. There are more magazines, more celebrities – so the whole thing has been watered down.

"And there is a lot of cock out there."

Leibovitz, as the master of her own "school" of photography, says she has now turned to a more sophisticated use of ideas.

Early pictures of Leibovitz's family are included in the exhibition. She spent much of her early life travelling across the US with her five brothers and sisters. Her mother was a New York dancer (Leibovitz remains interested in dance photography). Her father was a colonel in the US Air Force, and the family moved from base to base, with Leibovitz in the back of the car, viewing America through a window frame.

She started learning photography in 1968 at the San Francisco Art School, submitting some work to the young Rolling Stone magazine and being given her first assignment. Soon she was on the staff and on the road, covering the greatest moments and people of the day.

"Rolling Stone wasn't really commercial like today," she says. "You felt that what you did mattered and was important."

Then Mick Jagger invited her to cover a Rolling Stones band tour, which led to a much-publicised slide into a drug habit for her. It was serious, but, she has said, the work saved her.

The Work is a phrase Leibovitz uses often. It is all-important. "My best friend has been my work. My best friendship. It has been the most remarkable. It's a 'constant' and I get a lot from it.

"I don't really have time for friends, and the few friends I have have stayed with me because they don't give up. They just keep on calling.

"I am actually not a good friend to have because I can't be there at the most important times. I am very committed to my brothers and sisters and my parents and try to be there to see them.

"I don't want to be 70 years old and walking around with bags of negatives ... 'there she is again ... it's her with those bags of negatives ...'

"But the people I work with are wonderful people and I have worked hard to get a nice group. I have discovered I like nice people better than if they are good. It sounds a little corny, but it works. And they work really hard."

So what about talk of her being hard to work for?

"I'm horrible. Pretty bad. Better."

Mmmm.

"Really, I am better than I have ever been. I think a lot of that came from not working with people. I spent the first eight or 10 years of my working life by myself. Then I had assistants and I couldn't understand why they didn't just get it.

"It has taken years to learn how to work with people.

"I am just getting better now ..."

§   §   §   §   §

Somewhere deep inside, there is something comfortable about Annie Leibovitz these days. And it's not a word I had expected to associate with her.

It is perhaps something to do with a small room at the end of the studio. In there are file upon black file of photographic material, 10 shelves deep, covering two walls, floor to ceiling. Over 18 months, archivist Carolyn Kass has meticulously filed Annie Leibovitz's work from the 80s and 90s. Some 1500 shoots tucked away in the computer. A priceless record of social taste and change. (Kass points to five black filing cabinets apprehensively. "I haven't started on the 70s yet.")

It is the Body of Work to which Leibovitz refers often.

"I think the strength of the work is the body of work," she says. "I love it when I take a good picture, which is a few times a year. I love photography. I love it when it works. I still get excited. It just gets more interesting because you have a body of work. You know that to keep adding to it makes it more and more interesting."

Her first recognition of the importance of the Body of Work seems to have come during work on her book Photographs, Annie Leibovitz 1970 – 1990, and its subsequent exhibition.

(The exhibition made her only the second living photographer to be granted a retrospective show at the Smithsonian's National Portrait Gallery in Washington. The other was Irving Penn, who had to wait until he was 72. Leibovitz was 41 – young for a "retrospective".)

Compiling the book and exhibition seems also to have marked a personal turning point.

She says putting the book and exhibition together was "an extraordinary exercise in looking at the work and making decisions that I have now put into action". She decided to do more of the reportage work that comprised her early assignments for Rolling Stone magazine 26 years before.

It led to simpler portrait work, like pictures at a shelter for abused women, for The New Yorker magazine. Black and white. One assistant loading cameras. One light.

Shooting O.J. Simpson's portrait, she also had just one assistant.

She even sees it as the start of the process which has led to the simpler line-and-form Olympics.

"Then once or twice a year I have to just take my camera." Like that, she has visited Sarajevo and Rwanda.

But the refocusing has been painful.

"I realise I have become a less good reportage photographer than when I was young and naive and innocent. The Rwanda photographs weren't great photographs. They were OK pictures. I was disappointed.

"You can't do portrait work and that work, and I have become a better portraitist and I have had to let it go – that has been a little painful to have to admit."

She also had to assess her own way of doing things as she progressed through her mid-40s.

"It is really important, as every artist knows, that you have to take care of your time and your talent. It's like a baby and it has to be fed and taken care of and rested. If you do anything long enough you learn when you are getting dangerously close to burning yourself out.

"One of the nicest things about getting older is that things slow down naturally. There's something really nice about it. You just do things slower. You can't go, go, go."

She says this and yet admits: "I have just been through a period when I thought it's worse than it's ever been." So she sent out the order: "Cancel Ralph Lauren. I can't do it! I don't want to take a bad picture." But the shoot had already been set up and she went through with it. ("There is something to be said for just doing it.")

This doesn't seem to quite add up, I point out.

"I think I am busier now, but I use my time better," she says. And she is perhaps calmer, more measured, less frenetic.

She is also taking August off. "I plan pretty much to stay still. I have decided to do this as often as I can for the rest of my life, because one needs more time to renourish the cells. You are not only doing it for yourself, but for the work."

If the book and exhibition brought a realisation of the Body of Work, the book tour which followed brought a realisation of what the work meant to others.

"I worked for many, many years in a vacuum," she says. "I did the work and was not quite aware of any kind of audience to the work. People have always known my photographs more than they have known me."

The Body of Work has bought a Body of Wealth. It has long been whispered that hiring Leibovitz and entourage costs well over $US50,000 a day. Her annual contract with Conde Nast is said to be worth another $1m, and other deals are highly lucrative.

She declares (a little unconvincingly): "I don't think I am the best paid photographer in the world."

But adds: "I think I am paid very well.

"I don't want to be a stupid businesswoman, but I am not really sharp when it comes to business.

"I have been at this for 26 years. I do know what I am doing and I don't listen to people who tell me what to do, because they don't know what they are talking about – and they have to pay me for that.

"I think it's more apparent than ever that they are trying to sell magazines, so they should pay me well. If they were in a different mode – trying to do great art – I would go right in line and not ask to be paid well."

She adds: "No one wants to be taken advantage of. I worked at Rolling Stone for 13 years and Jann and Jane Wenner were getting more houses and cars and their lifestyle was getting more lavish and I had felt I was an integral part of their look for those years.

"I have no complaints, but at a certain point ... well, they are selling magazines – they should share it. Magazines make a certain amount of money.

"I have a lot of extraordinary opportunities," she says. "It seems like the ante gets upped every time. It's a lot of responsibility and I have worked very hard."

She pauses: "But I am doing what I want to do now. The work is diverse – from Cuba to Sir Anthony Hopkins. I am in a very, very, very lucky place. I wish I had more years and more time."

Up in the Air

RICHARD WOLDENDORP IS ONE of the world's finest aerial photographers. He has flown thousands of hours over the cities and suburbs, coastlines and deserts of Australia, and other countries. With his heavy glass lenses and faultless eye, he paints the continent's remarkable landscape as Aborigines usually do, from above. He charts waterholes, animal tracks, landscape with the broadest brush.

He prefers to fly with pilots he knows – whom he has shown examples of the way he photographs so they have an understanding of what he is aiming for.

I should have remembered this about an hour ago. Things on this aerial photography assignment in the north of Australia started to go wrong then, when the plane wouldn't start.

When most mechanical contrivances won't start, you know because of the silence. If a single-engined plane decides not to start, it seems, you know because of the noise. There is a constant winding of the starter, as the pilot tries to whip the little lawnmower engine into a momentum that will result in spark-and-combustion. (It reminds me of a friend's philosophy on rope-pull started outboard motors – that they store the energy put into them to release randomly, at a time and place of their own choosing).

The frenzy worked. The engine caught, coughed, spat out a cloud of blue smoke. Stopped, caught again, revved hard and then settled to a windy buzz. I checked my lap strap and looked out of the hole where there used to be a door (the pilot had happily removed the pins from its two little hinges, and lifted it off for the purposes of the photography). The rough texture of the gravel taxiing strip became smooth and milky as we grunted from stationary to slow movement.

We drove around the little airport for a while, looking for a nice, empty piece of bitumen. The pilot seemed quite happy doing this. With the door off, the plane sounded like a World War I fighter. Somewhat haphazardly, it seemed, he went through a mental checklist, wiggling the steering wheel, glancing over dials, occasionally glancing out at the wings.

Yep, she'd do.

Then, through the gobby black microphone touching his bottom lip, he called the Control Tower. "G'day." Somehow this familiarity vaguely concerned me. It seemed somehow too chatty. "You get home alright?" I liked the implication of this even less. "I woke up with a bull roaring in me guts, but I'm coming good."

By now I am, purposely, quite mesmerised by the glistening bitumen. I have removed myself from this conversation. Quite frankly, I don't want to know.

"OK then. We'll be a couple of hours I guess. Just flying around the town and out over the ocean a bit."

Too chatty by far.

Bitumen flying past my naked skin doesn't bother me (I ride motorcycles). In fact, I have always been rather entranced by it. It is somehow threatening, yet somehow distant. Although I know from experience how unpleasant contact with it can be (I fall off motorcycles), it seems so removed that it doesn't quite count. It reminds me of the Starship Enterprise when, at Warp Factor 4 or so, the stars she is passing become streaked and blurred. (Scotty echoes around the cockpit: "She canna take anymore, Cap'n. She's ferlin apart at thu sims." In fact, when motorcycling, I have been known to quote him loudly, inside my fullface helmet, on particularly fast bends.)

The bitumen is now blurred and the pilot is whistling a Grateful Dead tune. My concern grows. But, we are on our way. Sort of. I like being hermetically sealed in big jets. I like the strapping down procedure. I like them Arming Doors and Cross Checking. I like the dong-dong-dong of the No Smoking warning. I like being shown the little light on the shoulder of the lifejacket, though I have always doubted its use in attracting grid-search aircraft to me. Or the orange plastic whistle for bringing over the nearest frigate ("Captain, this is the Bridge. Sorry to wake you, but we can hear a whistle out there somewhere ... ") Still, I like the sheer controlled drama of it all. And most of all, I like the kick in the back as they open her up at the start of the runway and the jets catapult you forwards, and up towards the sky. It seems, well, a fitting way to leave the ground.

This plane isn't at all like that. The pilot opens her up, alright, but the noise increase is not incrementally linked to the increase in speed. Nevertheless, she slowly builds up, until we are tonking along at quite a brisk pace, just waiting for a fortuitous puff of wind under our wings to lift us into the sky. It doesn't come and, as we drive past the tower, I wonder whether the end of the runway will come before the puff of wind. I wonder when something will happen. Indeed, it does. The engine stops. It just lays down and dies right there in its tracks. The pilot looks sideways at me. Shrugs. Calls his mate in the tower and tells him, and arranges for a tow back to the hangar.

Never mind, he says, we'll use another plane.

Good idea.

So we drag all the gear out and move to a snazzy little blue number and I wait around the hangar while the pilot takes the door off. We jump in and I am, by now, hot and bothered. The pilot turns the key. The engine reluctantly drags itself through a complete revolution in slo-mo. Wer-wer-wer. There is no sign of a spark. He turns the key again. Nothing. The battery is flat.

"The battery's flat."

Thanks. Thanks very much for clarifying that. To be honest, I am only brave enough to think this, not voice it, on the off-chance that we should, at some juncture, actually get into the air, putting my life unquestionably in the pilot's hands.

He calls his mate at the tower again. "Hi. The battery's flat. Yep … Yep … Yep."

I am waiting for the little towing buggy with the long arm to come and retrieve us once again, but it doesn't appear. In its place is a man who looks vaguely like a mechanic (dirty overalls, orange cap, workboots) pushing a trolley holding a battery pack and two leads. He walks half the length of the runway, whistling, to where we are stationary, nods G'day, hooks the plane up and signals the pilot to have a go. The engine turns over interminably – almost to the point of flattening the battery pack – before spluttering into life and then revving hard again.

Almost before we are uncoupled, we are on our way, driving back down the runway past the control tower, before turning and taking the big run-up again. The plane coughs a couple of times during this procedure, but a puff of wind comes just before we run off the bitumen and onto the grass and we shoot up, as if some ground-mounted fan were driving us vertically into the sky.

The engine settles into a bored, ineffective sort of hum.

By now, though, cloud is starting to come over. For aerial photography, you don't just want a clear day, you want a perfect day. Absolute clarity, the finest light. Then things will work out. Less than this and you are shooting through the gauze of atmosphere.

But I can't break this to the pilot. It's better to just do what's possible, and get back down. Going through the motions, risking shooting at 125th of a second, which may not be a fast enough exposure to prevent movement blurring the image, but will expose the film better for colour, there isn't much hope of anything great coming from this flight. But there is a consolation. As the little wheels bite back into the bitumen, I am, at least, still alive.

Aerial photographers have their own recipes, and some guard them closely. But, as you will have gathered, there are some simple rules. Only shoot in perfect conditions – don't accept anything less, even if it means dragging a pilot from bed four dawns in a row to tell him the flight is off. Don't shoot at less than 125th of a second. Have the door taken off the plane (make sure there is a proper full harness). Make sure the plane has high wings. Use a helicopter where you can – they can hover in one spot and give you longer to shoot. Find good pilots and stick with them as much as possible – they will come to know what you are looking for, will put you where you want to be, then drift past the subject matter.

Parts of the south coast of Australia are renowned for their white sand and ocean of the most exquisite turquoise, deepening to a royal blue. Bays are often carved into wine-glass curves, and islands provide breathtaking material for aerial photography.

Today's pilot has never flown a photographer before. He has recently taken up his flying career, but has mostly been delivering seafood. There are advantages in this cargo – seafood doesn't get airsick (I don't think), doesn't scare easy and doesn't complain. Perfect passengers for his flying style.

I am not a univalve. The pilot manages to distress me from the outset. His moleskin pants hang low around his rear, strapped under a paunch with a brown leather belt which carries a small knife holder. In some places his old checked shirt is tucked in, in some places not (I like pilots with neat minds).

No, he has too much devil-may-care – or perhaps sloppiness – about him. He positively drools at the opportunity to fly with the door off. Nevertheless, up we go. The takeoff is faultless, and he climbs to a low cruising height without even thinking about it. The pilot knows how to fly, alright. But there's something about him that bothers me. I gradually work out that he enjoys it just a little TOO much. (I prefer a vague air of boredom in my pilots.)

"Perhaps we could go down and do some shots of that bay," I suggest, never sure exactly where the microphone should be to be voice activated, or how loud I should shout over the whine of the engine and the thunder of the wind. He hears me, alright. But rather than banking around to present the open doorway to the subject matter, and slowly drifting past, he points the noise of the plane at the sand, opens up the throttle and powers down towards it.

"Aaaaaaaarrrrrrgggggggghhhhhhhhhh!!!!!!!!!!!!!!!!" My hands are spread across my face. There is a small gap between the index and middle fingers of the left hand because, despite not wanting to see where I am going or how fast, I have a sneaking curiosity about where I am going to die. The Starship Enterprise is at Warp Factor 4 and the stars are blurred. In seconds, the sand has closed to the point where I can pick out individual grains.

I have forgotten about cameras, lenses, f-stops and exposure. To hell with aerial photography. I am going to die. I am going to die. I am going to die. This dumb maniac of a seafood deliverer is going to plunge us both so deeply into the sand that we may never be found, until an archaeologist several generations from now finds us embedded and fossilised in a sandstone ridge and wonders why one of the skeletons has its hands around the other's throat.

To hell with you. And thanks very much.

With a "Wwwhhhhheeeeeeeeeeeeeeeee" sound resembling that from a thrilled child on a swing, he pulls her up, the wheels narrowly missing the sand. We are pulling so many Gs, I can't help but smile.

"Get anything?"

The pilot has a strange notion of aerial photography. He somehow seems to imagine it is possible to point the lens of a camera through the scratched, domed perspex window of a Cessna in a death dive and capture perfect, detailed, emotional images, even when the view is partially obscured by a multi-dialled dashboard, and there's sun flaring across the white paintwork. No, it just doesn't work like that.

"Er, no. Perhaps we could go back up and have another go at it." And so we climb back up to 200 metres, and he circles once. "Now look, that bay's really good, but that just wasn't the way to do it. I just want you to set me up, with the door facing it, and all the wing and stuff out of the way, at about 100m, then drift past. Take it really slowly and keep the plane level and as still as you can."

"AAAAAAAAAAAAAAAAaaaaaaaaaaaaaaaaaaaaaaarrrrrrrrrrrrrrrr rrgggggggggggghhhhhhhhhhh!!!!!!!!!!!!!!!!!!"

My belief that I have never really mastered the intricacies of the voice-activated microphone are thus proven. My hands are spread across my face. There is a small gap between the index and middle fingers. I am going to die. I am going to die. I am going to die.

He never did get it right. And I got only a few snatched images.

Another Australian aerial photographer, Rod Taylor, did better under duress during a long assignment in the remote Kimberley region, in the north-west of the continent. His assignment began with doubts as he loaded his equipment into a tired-looking, very small helicopter. It got worse after they took off. As they settled into a cruising speed in the glass bubble, the pilot looked at him with concern and asked: "Can you hear a funny noise?"

This is not a comforting thing for a pilot to ask, under any circumstances.

They carried on and, during the trip, dropped into a deep gorge to photograph a waterfall, in full flood during the Wet Season. They hovered around in the spray while Rod shot his images. Then he nodded to the pilot. They continued to hover around in the spray. Rod signalled that he'd finished. They continued to hover round in the spray. Rod signalled the pilot to take her up.

But the chopper, with its tired old rotors, hadn't enough lift to get them out of the gorge. Fortunately a gust of wind eventually helped to push them up and out.

But helicopters can make a very good platform for aerial photography. One Perth pilot was a dab hand at it. He could set it up and just drift past while you sat quietly exposing film, taking light readings, adjusting cameras, changing lenses, working the subject matter. It was all very low-key, very relaxing. Very dreamy. The images were perfect.

I remembered Richard Woldendorp's advice. Find a pilot who can do it and stick with him. For the next assignment, I rang to book the same helicopter pilot. They were sorry, he couldn't do it. In fact, he was in hospital. He'd survived the crash, but he didn't think he'd fly any more.

§   §   §   §   §

Richard Woldendorp says that in the bush, you have to take "anything that flies". He says bush pilots often have the knowledge and an interest in the area being photographed.

"Some fly a plane like they are riding a horse. I like that freedom in a pilot, in order to get my shots."

Flying with your feet on the ground

THE TRICK, says Captain John Dennis, is to keep your eyes firmly fixed on the end of the runway. The far-distant spot where it disappears. It makes steering a Boeing 747-400 with your toes that much easier.

The Trick, in fact, works rather well. The 747 (you don't hear the dumbo word Jumbo round the Qantas Jet Base in Sydney) tracks pretty straight down the dotted white line marking the centre of the runway, your toes twiddling away on the pedals.

Some 398 tonnes of tubing containing nearly 426 lives at 200kmh all resting on the corn of a big toe.

C'mon Maverick. Take it easy. Settle. This is serious. This is Top Gun school. At 300kmh, Captain Dennis gives the order to ease back the controls and pull the nose in the air, pointing it up by 12 and a half degrees (of necessity, he's a specific man).

"Hokeydokley."

"Just watch the Attitude," he tells me.

I have been told this before.

Amazed, and not a little depressed, that my personality is so transparent that it can earn me a warning from a virtual stranger, I can only reply: "I've always had a problem with attitude."

"No, the plane's. That's its angle. The angle of its ascent. That's its Attitude."

"I knew that."

Captain Dennis looks at me as if suspecting that the first interpretation may, in fact, have been the more accurate.

The nose rises and the wheels smoothly lift from the tarmac. Textbook stuff. Wouldn't even spill the orange juice from a plastic cup.

"You've lost an engine." Captain Dennis's calm voice interrupts my moment of supreme pride.

I am tempted to reply "How frightfully careless of me," but feel the Humour Thing may have already had its day.

Anyway, when you are staring into a screen trying to keep a funny little square on a particular horizontal line, and a triangle pointing downwards at a vertical line and your airspeed constant, there really is no opportunity to look dramatically out of the window of a 747 to see precisely which of the four massive jet engines you have lost. Or whether anyone was underneath at the time.

Good job there are all those warning lights, bedecking the flight deck's ceiling like fluoro stars on a kid's bedroom ceiling.

Losing an engine during a 747-400's takeoff has a marked effect. Now having twice as much power on one side as the other, the plane "torques" and veers off hard in one direction. The sheer grunt feels like it is trying to slap you onto the ground, on your side, damned hard. Captain Dennis has already told me what to do in this instance and I jam my left foot on the rudder to compensate. "Smoothly but firmly." You betcha.

There are congratulatory murmurs on the flight deck. Those strapped in around me seem suitably impressed. Go Maverick.

"The most important thing is to keep that rudder on," continues Captain Dennis, mixing calmness with continued warning. "Don't let it off at all. Continue the ascent. Watch your speed. Watch your course. And watch your Attitude."

I start humming the theme tune from Top Gun under my breath ... I wish I hadn't lent the Ray Bans to a friend ... I wish I had worked out, so I could fill a crisp white t-shirt better ... I wish I had Tom Cruise's money ...

What is amazing about this whole scenario is that, in fact, it is not a 747-400 at all. It is a white box on six hydraulic legs in a big room in Sydney with a huge umbilical cord connecting it to the outside world. This Qantas flight simulator is worth $35 million and costs $1000 an hour to run. It works around the clock, and getting to "fly" one, it is continually stressed to me, is a rare and very special privilege.

The simulators exactly replicate the performance, reactions and handling of an aircraft. Even sitting on the runway, you feel that familiar "bobbling" effect as the plane ticks over. Effectively, for the pilots and first officers, they ARE real aircraft. If you can fly a simulator, you can fly the real thing.

Fed into them are incredibly life-like, and completely accurate, three-dimensional representations of the world's airports. Flying into Hong Kong, you can see the boats in the harbour, skyscrapers, the mountains. The familiar sights around Sydney. And today, London Heathrow is even more life-like.

"Not much of a day," says Captain Dennis, prodding at a screen (interestingly labelled "This Touch Screen is for Fingers Only"). Visibility drops to 100m (in Australia you can only land in visibility of up to 600m, as we have less highly calibrated navigation systems, he says).

"Oh, and it's dusk." Another touch of the screen, to make the landing even trickier.

In fact, the three autopilots will fly the plane in "blind" – you only see the tarmac when it's 9.1m below you. All the way down to 6m, you can still abort a landing and pull out. After that you're committed. (And probably should be.)

Within the Qantas Jet Base Flight Training Facility there are, in fact, eight units – three 747-400s, two 747-300s, two 767s and a Dash 8.

Here Qantas pilots are carefully and thoroughly trained, to take up the mantle of continuing to make it "the world's safest airline."

It is one of the most revered training facilities going (and also used to train Ansett 747 pilots). And Captain John Dennis, Qantas' Customer Liaison Captain, Flight Operations, is one of the most revered pilots. He joined Qantas in 1971 and has 12,000 hours under his belt, some 6000 in command of 747-400s. He flies prestige and inaugural flights ... to the Antarctic, and the first Qantas flight into New York.

For all this, he is a friendly and unassuming man. Albeit with a rather unusual repertoire in practical jokes.

Having averted the disaster of ripping up the grass at Sydney airport (not to mention losing countless hundred lives), he cooks up something else.

"Ease the speed back."

I pull the four throttles back.

"And more ... "

And back further.

"And more ..."

The controls start to shake violently (apparently a neat Aussie invention to warn pilots of impending doom).

"It's stalling."

Oh terrific. Thanks for that.

Captain Dennis talks me through the recovery from this precarious situation.

Throughout a three hour session in the simulator, he talks "pilots" through everything from an engine fire to (most remarkably to me) the loss of one, then two, then three engines. I say remarkable because the plane still flies. On one engine. Up to 400 tonnes of her. It will even accelerate and climb.

I remember, at this point, thinking it would take a special talent to crash a 747. They strike me as incredible machines.

Captain Dennis confirms this amateur opinion of the plane. He turns to me. Grins. "It's flying perfectly. It's a GREAT machine." And somehow he conveys not only his continued great love of, and enthusiasm for, flying, but also his particular love of the 747.

It's a funny thing. Back in the tube of a 747 is a world of foiled fodder, endless movies and meaningless magazines. And waiting. (A world suitably paired with the world of the airport ... of queues and baggage checks. And waiting.) A world where you live with someone's head in your lap and their chair crushed against your knees. Where I display a special talent for reserving the seat next to a crying toddler and frantic parents. It has always seemed to me to be very far removed from the philosophical, romantic (and physical) notion of flight.

The flight deck, however, is quite different. It is part of a real aircraft. A real, responsive aircraft that you actually have to fly. "People think the 747 is a big, lumbering giant. It's not," says Captain Dennis. "But you have got to think ahead all the time. It's like playing a game of chess. You have to be thinking a long way ahead of the aircraft."

The ability to anticipate and handle conditions and problems comes from training. And that's what passengers around the world buy as part of their cost of their air ticket. They invest in these simulators and men like Captain John Dennis.

They also invest in facilities like the Qantas Jet Base itself, shown to us in detail by heavy maintenance manager Peter Hulskamp ("Maintenance Supervisor, Aircraft Recovery Coordinator") ... a man full of pride in the 747, in Qantas itself, and in its workshops.

Not that some of them look like workshops at all. The Avionics Clean Room looks more like a cross between a hospital operating theatre and an administration office. In this pristine environment, the more sensitive parts of the 747's entrails are cared for. The air is filtered, and the environment dust-free.

In the huge hangars, 747s are wheeled in and propped up on three jacks (one under the tail, one under each wing). "To see a 747 jacked up above you is just AWESOME," says Mr Hulskamp.

The parts you see lying around the place are enough to send anyone with even the vaguest technical bent into a spin. Especially the fan from the 747's Rolls Royce engines. It revolves at 3500 rpm and produces most of the power in the engine (each 6cm x 3cm blade produces more power than a Formula One race car). Yet it is so finely balanced, the stationary fan can be turned by a single finger.

Aircraft come in for maintenance work (a hail storm in Sydney, with ice the size of tennis balls, sparked the biggest repair program ever) and for rebuilds that may take many weeks. The care put into the fleet is reflected in the demand for used Qantas planes – "they are snapped up by other airlines," explains Mr Hulskamp.

"Everything is repairable," he says. "But it is always safety and quality first. There is no doubt about that."

This philosophy is echoed throughout the simulator complex. All of which has given Qantas 19 million passengers annually, in 139 aircraft (100 in the main Qantas fleet, the others flown by subsidiary airlines) serving 104 destinations, 50 in Australia.

And services that continue to grow, with increasing numbers of 747-400 flights even domestically around Australia. They give passengers more facilities and the 747 has the particular advantage of offering Business and First Class passengers more comfort than on smaller planes.

It's funny we should get round to the subject of smaller planes.

Because there's one heading for us now.

Right for us.

The 747-400's radar shows a plane tracking straight at us. Fast. Bloody fast.

There are a number of audible warning systems in the cockpit of a 747, all with a calm male voice. Interestingly, only one has a female voice. This is in the Terminal Collision Avoidance System – the system that tells you there's another plane coming straight at you ... nose to nose.

"TRAFFIC! TRAFFIC!" She says, with discernible force. We duck fast under the oncoming jet and watch it swoop overhead.

But why a female voice? Well, it certainly makes the mostly-male pilots listen and respond. Really respond.

"CLEAR OF CONFLICT," she announces.

Goodo, Hun.

In the Desert

*Voyaging through the interior of Australia takes you
back into history ... and forward to the future.*

YOUR MIND IS FILLED WITH GOLD. The oceans of spinifex
ruffle and swagger in the desert breeze, deepening in colour with
the lowering sun. "Oceans" is a good word   they are fluid as water
and with as many quickly changing moods. (After dusk the spinifex
becomes pale and milky-gold, like a low, cold mist washing round
dramatic islands of desert oaks.)

The landscape out here follows ancient seabeds. The journey
south through four of Western Australia's deserts transect great
oceans which, two billion years before, saw stromatolites pumping
out oxygen, creating an atmosphere in which we could live. Setting
up the chemical formula which would make iron oxide turn the

land red. Before India was ripped from the Australian continent.

The oceans of spinifex roll over a thousand dunes, regular as waves, peaking, troughing in swales. The face steep, the back less so, and drifting away, driven flatter by wind. Just like water waves.

Gold, red and orange dominate the landscape, and your sight, through the Tanami, Great Sandy, Gibson and Little Sandy deserts. We are following landscape and an idea, following Aboriginal myth and rock-wall reminders, and the trails of early white explorers. A couple of thousand kilometres through the very essence of remoteness.

Salt lakes. Mud pans. Dunes. The wriggly remains of trees. A bonsai landscape of endless plant varieties.

Already the demands of description have climbed all over the mind and driven out words in a fancy exhibition. Space and landscape, horizon and time, journey and quest, and the desire to share it all.

The effect is particularly acute in desert regions. And particularly in Western Australia's epic and picturesque interior. If God has a garden – any god, I don't mind which – this is it. A garden manicured by the elements, by heat, wind and the scarcity of water. Gardened to eye-level, as we ourselves garden.

This is a world so organic it makes you feel like a human being – an elemental, simplified, easily satisfied, grateful, appreciative, awed, less-damaging human being; not a consumer, not sophisticated, not driven by want. Quickly quite different.

But is it a modern phenomenon to see the interior this way? Is it a modern phenomenon to romanticise space and vastness and horizon? Are we so squashed up that space ... any sort of space ... is appealing?

It may be. Listen to David Carnegie (later the Honourable). He was 21 in 1892 when he arrived from England to join the Goldrush. Two years later he led his first expedition into the desert regions, and in 1896-97, he made it, by this route, to the Kimberley.

In the introduction to his account of that journey, he says the traveller in the Australian bush has "no beautiful scenery, broad lakes, or winding rivers to make life pleasant for him. The unbroken monotony of an arid, uninteresting country has to be faced. Nature everywhere demands his toil. Unless he has within him impulses that give him courage to go on, he will soon return; for he will find nothing in his surroundings to act as an incentive to tempt him further."

Carnegie was looking for a route through the deserts, on foot, on camel, living on his wits and skills, living by the will of God, living by luck.

You can't compare it to a journey by four-wheel-drive, with navigation and radio equipment and a map on your knee – and the wells sunk by Alfred Canning in 1908. I know that. But words like "monotony" and "uninteresting" have nothing to do with any of these things.

They have nothing to do with, much later, the words of John Forrest (later Lord) in his own diary. The sandhills, he wrote, represent "nothing but desolation".

They have to do with emotion.

Comfort is a factor, but so is the shift in our perceptions. Somewhere between the early descriptions and today's appreciation of space is Max Dupain's pivotal photograph, Sunbaker, which was taken in 1937 and is held by the Australian National Gallery in Canberra.

The photograph is of a man, lying face down on sand. He is tanned to darkness, relaxed in his environment. This iconic photograph has become pivotal in Australian history.

Let me quote from Gael Newton's authoritative book on Australian photography, Shades of Light: "Made at the time of the sesquicentenary, the Sunbaker was also an image of ownership of the land: the white man is nearly black, and safe within his environment that he can lie face down."

I don't think Newton meant "ownership" of the land in the legal sense. I take it to mean "ownership" in modern-speak. The sunbaker is comfortable with and feels committed to the land. He is at home.

I have some Aboriginal friends who will feel uncomfortable with this, who see people of European heritage as invaders. I have other Aboriginal friends who will feel happy that white people are on the journey towards understanding and appreciating – and therefore caring for – this land as their ancestors did.

Shifts of perception are not easy.

I am travelling the deserts from the Kimberley to the Goldfields – 2000km of varied, intriguing, vegetated landscape – with others. A senior Australian, born here, tells me this: "Attitudes in 1999 are totally different to even 30 or 40 years ago."

Do you think we are more romantic? "Spiritual rather than romantic. Aborigines talk about it being their land – I think a lot of whites are feeling this, if in a different way. I think a lot of Australians are like it without being able to articulate it."

Over recent years I have constantly been told, read and heard Aborigines stating that they feel it is time to share their stories and understandings of this land (I have just been invited to attend a secret Aboriginal ceremony, for this purpose). Forget Canberra. Perhaps there is another form of reconciliation possible.

The people I am with become awed by the landscape. "I have never had experience of sand ridge country. I really think it is beautiful. The feeling of isolation and wonder."

Another: "I have just been drinking in the aura of it."

Sound like a bunch of whackos? They're not. The people I quote are a retired lady researcher, a retired wood machinist and a horticulturist.

Another four-wheel-drive pulls in near our camping spot one night and a bloke wanders over to say g'day. "Just being neighbourly." He's a work-a-day sort, but he talks animatedly about the difference between each of the swales (the "valleys" between each dune). As you come over the crest, each swale seems subtly but noticeably different in vegetation and mood.

It is remarkable to see nature working as it should. It is remarkable to see land that isn't obviously trashed (although feral cats are changing the patterns of small fauna).

Most of all, I find it remarkable that I find this remarkable.

The trees. The desert oak trees. First they are small, whispy things. Then they thicken to elegant pencils. When they are mature, they widen out to a quite different shape – big trunked, big branched. A "traditional" tree and extremely pretty.

And here, in this landscape, you see them all together – young trees naturally seeding, growing alongside older trees. Progression. Replacement. Regeneration. Recruitment. It is all working properly – sustainably. Each tree is part of an ongoing cycle. You can see a future here. You can see how it is all meant to happen. How it is all supposed to work. Forever.

Somehow this is not part of our everyday world. We don't often see land that isn't farmed or shaped or managed or interfered with. Land where a seed can fall and germinate and grow as it should and, given time, replace the tree from which it has fallen. Where forests sprout up of their own volition. Where there are no stock or crop or tourist activities to stop this recruitment.

I find I don't want to tell people where these places are. A botanist I am with thinks this wrong – that education and knowledge mean we will care for these places and protect them. He may be right. But instinctively I feel that even a few people visiting here would bring about untold, irreparable environmental damage. It would interfere with this natural cycling. (I camped the first night in the Kimberley before heading into the desert surrounded by human faeces and toilet paper.)

That I have no faith is, I feel, a shocking indictment. What a species.

Each of the four deserts are quite different, and not like the Sahara at all. These are old deserts, not "all sand" but covered with very varied vegetation and quite beautiful.

A horticulturist in the group says he likes desert regions because the plants are low: knee-height, small trees, big shrubs. Much as we create our domestic gardens. Everything at viewing level, not lost in some high canopy.

The canopy here comes after the golden, burning sun exits the big desert sky, dropping over the edge of this massive landscape, and making it look suddenly empty. The Moon rises with Venus, just like the tattoo on my shoulder. I count three, four shooting stars ... but can't relate this to the death of something so big or so far away. One night we all watch a feathery-tailed meteor come steaming in, horizontal.

"Look. A meteor."

"Could be a budgie with a headtorch."

I don't feel exposed out here. I don't feel anything is out of the ordinary. I lie in our drover's circle of swags around the fire, and feel this is how it should be. I think that being a human being is simpler than we have all been led to believe.

The Robert Bogucki Incident

For 40 days, first Western Australian authorities, then an elite American search force, looked for Robert Bogucki ... a US tourist "lost" in the Australian desert.
Was Robert Bogucki a hero or a villain? A money-waster who caused more trouble than he was worth, or someone to be revered for his individualism and spirit?

"To whom it may concern,

My name is Robert Bogucki. I am planning to enter the desert at the Sandfire Roadhouse and walk to Fitzroy Crossing. I am carrying ample food and nutrients, and water for the first five days. I have made extensive enquiries so that I can then walk from water hole to water hole.

I am formally trained in survival techniques.

I have comprehensive maps and I am an expert navigator – I have equipment with me to enable me to take the shortest possible route (a map of this is attached). I have also completed a first aid course and I am carrying adequate first aid equipment. I will carry an EPIRB which I will activate should I require assistance.

I am fit and prepared and of sound mind. I am looking forward to the experience and challenge of the desert. I will contact you when I reach Fitzroy Crossing, and if not by the date on the chart attached, you may assume I need assistance and I would be grateful for this.

Yours sincerely ..."

ROBERT BOGUCKI NEVER WROTE THIS LETTER.

He never left a comprehensive route-planner, he didn't carry an electronic positioning beacon. He just walked into the desert. Why? Because that was the way he wanted it. He apparently wanted to travel through the desert in a simple way.

You and I might have only have tried venturing into the Great Sandy in four-wheel-drives with global positioning systems, a comprehensive set of spares and a bank of communications gear. That might be our way. It wasn't Bogucki's. And why should it be. After all, it's a free country isn't it? (And freedom of spirit is surely part of being in a free country.)

Well, yes. It is a free country to a point.

But mostly no. It's not. It's a very restrictive one.

By not leaving such a letter with the authorities, Robert Bogucki failed to conform to our society's demands for explanation, thoughtfulness, obsessive care of ourselves and, above all, the obtaining of permission.

He just trotted off on his own without a thought for all those people who would have to rescue him, whether or not he wanted it.

As I write, Andrew Harper is walking across the Tropic of Capricorn across the continent. He has communications equipment so that he can call for help. He has a satellite phone charged by solar power, so that he can regularly contact civilisation to say he's OK. He has three camels to carry all the gear. He has sponsorship, a web site and, by doing all of this, he has our permission.

Our paternalistic society's permission.

We don't want anyone dying out there.

In crossing the continent, Andrew Harper, he will be a record-breaker and a hero. Eighteen-year-old WA yachtsman David Dicks was too, because he made it solo round the world. And triple solo circumnavigator Jon Sanders and any other successful adventurers you may name.

The key word is successful. They are "heroes" if they are successful, "idiots" who need expensive rescue operations (like numerous European round-the-world yacht racers) if they are not.

And if Robert Bogucki had walked through the Great Sandy Desert simply and unaided, those that heard about it may have hailed him a hero too, if in a smaller way.

(The daring of the deed equals the volume of the applause).

But he wouldn't have been a record-breaker. To cross from Sandfire Roadhouse to Fitzroy Crossing in a straight line is about 500km. Tribal Aboriginal people travelled by foot in the Great Sandy Desert. Throughout our more recent history, prospectors, geologists, surveyors and fortune hunters have been out in our continent's remote places too.

They have all lived in the Outback ... the Aboriginal and the prospector ... for long periods. They prove it is possible to do so. No-one, in their time, thought to rescue them.

It was assumed that Robert Bogucki was lost, and he became something to be looked for. He became an exciting challenge. A Mission. We are obsessed by our own heroics, and our technologies.

Whether he was or wasn't lost is not the point ... we should think about our assumption that because someone hasn't checked in and got permission and followed instructions that we should go off after them.

Perhaps another "Robert Bogucki" might not be lost at all ... but know just where he is and simply want to be left alone. Perhaps he might just want to be in the desert for 40 days. Perhaps he might not even mind dying out there. Perhaps he might want to.

And there we step on the toes of another taboo.

It is OK to die in a medical facility. It's accepted that people will die in cars that no longer resemble cars but look more like beer cans after a testosterone-pumped youth has ripped them in half and mangled them.

But out there alone in one of the most beautiful deserts imagineable?

Hell no.

We can't handle that. That's straying dangerously close to euthanasia or suicide and these are subjects we are ill equipped to handle.

And we find it perhaps even harder to handle what may have been Robert Bogucki's Quest ... to travel not only into the Great Sandy Desert but into the darker and more colourful places of his mind. To embark on a spiritual journey, which may come from the isolation, or the power of place, or the sense of standing on the precipice between safety and danger.

To move onto another plane of thought and awareness and appreciation and understanding. To find an insight that may be quite inexplicable in another place, or another space.

What does all that mean?

That the spiritual journey may be more important than the physical. Spiritual? There will be much uncomfortable shuffling in seats over THAT word. Many – perhaps the majority – of our previous societies have been built on spiritualism of one form or another, yet it isn't often factored into our daily lives now.

It's taken to be a bit "soft" or "whacko". A bit dolphin-posters-and-pan-pipes-and-dream-catchers. So the idea of a spiritual journey is just too hippy. Yet, from the most ancient times to today, nature has been the catalyst in remarkable spiritual journeys. If we drop away the arrogance which has grown out of our perceived sophistication and technological powers, its the same for us as it was for our predecessors.

The whole notion of 40 days in the desert, being tested and seeking spiritual growth, is not new. New Testament, Luke 5:4: "And Jesus ... was led by the Spirit for 40 days in the wilderness, tempted by the devil. And he ate nothing in those days and when they were ended he was hungry ..." The devil tempted Jesus, and when those temptations were complete " ... Jesus returned in the power of the Spirit into Galilee."

The wilderness ... the desert ... was the backdrop for testing and greater insight. And so it is to this day, with the Men's Movement in the US, for example, largely growing from an epicentre in the Mexican desert.

Even with the four-wheel-drive and GPS and communications gear, there are still spiritual journeys going on in our deserts.

It is a journey into a world that Australian poet Les Murray once referred to in a seminar at La Trobe University. Another world. A world, he said, that not enough of us are prepared to experience. And through "the people's otherworld", he said, Australians could create an awareness of spirit and soul. (He even used this as a title for a volume of poetry in 1983.)

It has always been part of Aboriginal culture. "Aboriginal spirituality is primarily a spirituality of place," writes David J. Tacey, renowned lecturer and writer on the subject.

I am glad Robert Bogucki is alive, because this world needs all the people of individuality and spirit it can get. And people interested in taking spiritual journeys.

§　　§　　§　　§　　§

Having finished writing this, with a map of the Great Sandy Desert at my elbow, I notice for the first time some very fine, red writing on the edge of the desert:

"Read 'Aids to Survival' obtainable from Police Headquarters. Check with your automobile club, for information on spare parts, tools and equipment to be carried. Notify police of your intended journey and destination. Advise police of your arrival'."

The police have been advised. Robert Bogucki has arrived.

But to a hero's welcome?

The Cradle of Life

I HAVE BEEN TO THE CRADLE OF LIFE. I have seen the oldest dated life form on Earth. I have stood on the planet's most ancient crustal rocks. And I have been to the North Pole. All in the Pilbara, in arid Australia. All on one hot, sunny day.

I have taken the strangest journey back through time. Through three and a half billion years – a number that saturates the mind with zeros. My brain has grappled with, but probably not come even close to grasping, the enormity of the figure. Three and a half BILLION years. 3.5. Nought. Nought. Nought. Nought. Nought. Nought. Nought. Nought.

How does that compute against the mere 50,000 years of Aboriginal presence in Australia? Or the 2000 years since Christ? Or the 200 of contemporary Australian history?

They are like a flimsy topsoil dusting over the deep strata of the planet's history.

The North Pole expedition begins at remote Marble Bar not long after a perfect dawn. Professor George Seddon, geologist and author, has covered an outdoor table with maps and is describing the incredible underground form of the area we are about to visit (an area so precious we agree to keep its exact location secret).

The maps are a montage of colours – a geological textbook of strange phenomena all jammed on to one sheet. "It's a madman's breakfast," says the professor, with some excitement. "This is a paradise for rock hounds. You will see all forms of igneous rocks within 10 minutes' walk." And, for the sake of the botanists and horticulturalists present, he adds: "One thing geologists like about Western Australia is that it isn't too cluttered with plant cover."

While the party is very obviously thrilled by the novelty of visiting a place called the "North Pole", George is trying to drive home the true significance of the area. For it is here that the oldest known crustal rocks on Earth have been dated. And here that we will look for fossil stromatolites – the earliest recorded life on Earth.

For him, the geology and the stromatolites are of enormous importance – the fact that this was once a mine site that went by the name of "North Pole" is insignificant. The name was probably some fossicker's idea of a joke, but it provokes a flurry of questions. "Yes," says George. "The Earth's magnetic field has been flipped several times in the course of the planet's history, so that north and south reversed. And yes, polar wandering and continental drift mean that a point in the Pilbara could once have been polar. So this *could* have been the North Pole."

"However," he insists, "there is no evidence that it ever was."

(But it's a catchy story to tell in the pub. "So, what have you been up to today?" "Oh, I just popped up to the North Pole. Geez it was hot.")

"I wish people would get the North Pole subject out of the way," says George. "It's totally unimportant, geologically. We are now looking at the earliest part of the area's history. It's the oldest part and the most complex part. That's what is exciting about the area." George is a man generally given to understatement – or, at least, the accurate and well-measured statement.

The really significant part of the expedition, he explains, is the age of the rock and the fossil stromatolites.

The micro-organisms which created these stromatolites were single-celled, living in an atmosphere probably comprising carbon dioxide, nitrogen and methane ammonia.

What was it like then? "Steamy. Volcanoes erupting, cooling lava, shallow seas, igneous rocks, mostly granite, heaving away like hot, thick porridge down below. A reducing (deoxidising) atmosphere, mostly nitrogen and carbon dioxide, with traces of oxygen. Yet there was life, including cyanobacteria quietly building their layer-cake mushrooms of alternating sediment and organic films."

They would become photosynthetic, excreting oxygen. The professor explains that this oxygen combined with the abundant ferrous oxide dissolved in the sea water to give iron oxide. This process resulted in the huge iron deposits across the Pilbara.

It was also the start of the atmosphere as we know it – an atmosphere which could support myriad life forms.

In his book, Stromatolites, the Western Australian Museum's senior curator of invertebrate palaeontology, Ken McNamara, explains that such primitive-celled organisms have remained "virtually unchanged during the comings and goings of all the animals and plants that have ever lived."

They form complex communities, he says, which then form a very complex ecosystem. Evidence of these communities, such as fossil stromatolites in ancient rocks extending three-quarters of the way back to the origins of the solar system, represent the "oldest firmly established evidence for life on Earth".

The North Pole stromatolites "grew in an extensive, shallow sea into which lava erupted from nearby volcanoes. Scattered volcanic islands were also exuding lava into the sea. In the lowest sedimentary layer interbedded with these volcanic rocks, stromatolites occur."

The fossil stromatolites there today have been dated at three and a half billion years old. By comparison, those of the Napier Range (in the Kimberley) are just 360 million years old, and those at Hamelin Pool (Shark Bay) and Lake Richmond (near Rockingham) are living. And unchanged through the millennia.

But the novelty of a visit to the "North Pole" still wins out. Try as he might, in the interests of science, George has failed to dampen the excitement over it and, as we bump down an old goat track, it is talk of the North Pole that fills the four-wheel-drive.

"LOOK," someone screams, pointing.

"I think that's the North Pole. Over there." No, actually that's a cattle station homestead's antenna.

A little later, someone else: "LOOK. I've found it. Over there." No, that's a star picket stuck into a pile of rocks.

A selection of sticks along the roadside is greeted with more excitement.

This is just the sort of enthusiasm I've come to expect on the Kings Park and Botanic Garden expedition. While the group is primarily looking for plant life, this geological side trip has caused a stir.

But the Cradle of Life isn't quite that easy to find. While the bulk of the expedition stops for lunch, leader Luke Sweedman and fellow Kings Park staffer Grady Brand set out with a previous visitor's scribbled diary. Oh, and a global positioning system picking the brains of passing satellites.

They come back grinning. Soon we are all standing in a gently sloping valley, lightly covered with spinifex. This is it. The Cradle of Life.

Higher up, to the left, there is a chocolatey-brown outcrop of rock. The first fossil stromatolite we find. Higher up, on a saddle, a cluster of small domes. "We are incredibly privileged to see this," stresses George. "In a sense you are seeing the beginning of life. Never say where it is – the fossil stromatolites are terribly vulnerable."

Botanist Steve Forbes finds it hard to leave what he calls a "touchstone" of time.

It is only a couple of days later that I realise that my visit to the North Pole and fossil stromatolites has had a tangible impact on me. I'm just behind the professor, climbing down gorges in the Pilbara's Karijini National Park. I feel like I am in an elevator, descending through time to the bottom, laid two and a half billion years before. There is a real feeling of geological history. It is made more poignant by our recent days' travel through cattle country – land that upsets the botanists, who feel it has been "trashed" by hoofed beasts.

"But it's surviving," I reply, cheerfully. No, they say. There is no recruitment of young plants – anything that sticks its head up is eaten or trampled. When the existing trees and shrubs die, there will be nothing to replace them.

The bottom of the gorge feels like a secret valley – a moist micro-environment, seemingly landscaped, with birdsong filling the natural cathedral. Cooled by its permanent water, it has a magical quality. I look up the walls, through the millennia, and sense the degradation of our thin topsoil. Blowing away in the wind. I have been to the beginning of life, and now I sense its predicament ...

§ § § § §

Lying in my swag one night, staring up at the stars, for a moment I see the universe three dimensionally – not two – and feel I have the potential to understand all those noughts in three and a half billion years.

I think if you could truly comprehend time and space, and our relative place in it all, it could explode your brain. It just gives me a headache, so I pull the canvas over me and try to sleep.

§　　§　　§　　§　　§

Rare, Endangered and Going Critical

Extinction of a species is the stuff of science and fiction until it stares you in the face. Until you see a little cluster of plants on a hillside, hanging on for dear life. Or a stand of trees, seedless, with no young trees round them, knowing that when they have gone, the species is gone.

Trees trapped in a wheat paddock, surrounded by a chemical barrier. Unfenced and going nowhere.

Trees trapped on the land of a farmer who doesn't even have a vegie garden. Who hasn't even planted a few fruit trees. Who can't even feed his family. Who buys his carrots from town. Who has a paved front yard and a white concrete swan. Whose farm assistant says we wouldn't believe the volume of chemicals poured on this place. Who confides that they would feel safer living in a chemical industry area.

What hope, then, for Declared Rare Flora?

Extinction is just something you read about, until you mail off two cardboard boxes carefully filled with cuttings – being sent quickly back to the city for propagation. Labelled: "Express. Live plant material. With care. Next day delivery."

In the box are a handful of precious cuttings from *Grevillea batrachioides*. A DRF on the highest rung of the rare flora diving board. A Critical, from the last small community of 19 plants perched on the edge of extinction.

This pretty little grevillea bush with a delicate red flower was first described by botanist Ferdinand von Mueller, and noted in D.J. McGillivray's taxonomic revision in 1986. Then it vanished.

The species was presumed extinct until 1991, when the Grevillea Study Group found a sole population of 10 plants in the

Lesueur National Park, inland from Jurien on the Western Australian coast. But this information wasn't published until it appeared in The Grevillea Book, by Peter Olde and Neil Marriott, in 1995.

And even in 1993 in his taxonomic revision, D.J. McGillivray had to log the plant from a piece kept in storage. He reported: "Although I am reluctant to describe a new species from a single collection, in this instance it is done because the specimen appears to represent a distinct species that is possibly now extinct."

After the "find", Kings Park and Botanic Garden seed collector Luke Sweedman, armed with a special licence, went to collect seed in 1994, but the horticulturists were unable to propagate plants for the gardens or harvest seed for safe keeping in the garden's seed bank.

And when he found the population, he counted only seven plants. "The only population in the world. That's it."

Only a few people will ever know where *Grevillea batrachioides* is. It is protected by law and those who do know will keep the secret. And it is in a good place. Lesueur is recognised for its richness of flora − with 900 known species − and relatively unvisited.

Sweedman and I drive obscure sandtracks towards the area, then walk on in, through a soup of armpit-high plants. Wading gently into the varied mix of greens − mostly sharp stuff which rips at your pants.

Sweedman knows the general location, and remembers the slope. Remembers a rock. But finding so few plants when it's green to the horizon in every direction isn't so straightforward.

Then, suddenly, he stops. Not only have we found *Grevillea batrachioides*, but it is in flower.

This is the objective of our Quest, and the sharp end of the conservation argument. At my feet is a species once believed extinct. Now Critical. With its toes on the line.

Sweedman begins working his way around the area.

"Here's one."

"Here's another."

Then: "This small one is batrachioides too."

The word "small" is particularly significant. "Small" is, perhaps, the most important word on the Quest for *batrachioides*. For small means new plants. Recruitment, to use Sweedman's term.

Plants are temporarily tagged with orange tape, to make counting accurate. Fifteen mature plants, four juveniles. Nineteen in all. The species appears to be pulling its toes back from the line.

A small number of cuttings are carefully taken from nine plants (about one per cent of each plant, not enough to damage them), to give a broad gene pool. Last time he took cuttings from three – "I wanted to get the rest of the clones so I had a good cross-section of the genetic pool. If a fire went through and they didn't regenerate, we could reconstruct the population."

Sweedman is pleased by the appearance of new plants, which "indicates some regeneration." But I am still struck by the sea of green around me. Seven. Ten. Nineteen. Whatever. The odds against *Grevillea batrachioides*, which may have been a victim of some form of changed habitat or conditions, seem to me quite overwhelming. Impossibly so.

No-one can say why the population has reduced to remnant numbers. "There is something it doesn't like," says Sweedman. "It may have been more widespread at some time, but we don't know why it has been reduced to these numbers. It looks like it will be lost – but I am amazed that there are more plants."

Finding 19 healthy plants has cheered the pair, and I don't want to dampen the party – but I can only think of the grey file on the front seat of Sweedman's four-wheel-drive. I had leafed through it casually on the way north from Perth. Charts of plant details. Boxes with names, locations and numbers. Little numbers – a 10 or a six maybe.

It was only later that Sweedman explained that this is the DRF file. Some are Endangered, some Vulnerable, some Critical. The highest category. I read it more carefully, and feel quite hopeless. The plant numbers seem pathetic – the number of Criticals alone quite horrendous ... there are 95 Criticals. "Taxo (plants) facing an extremely high risk of extinction in the wild in the future," explains Sweedman. "All we know is that some populations are not recruiting because the habitat is changing."

But the list is also growing as knowledge about Western Australia's flora increases. "And WA probably knows more about its flora than other Australian states do about theirs."

We camp by a stream and listen to frogs.

The next day we continue the Quest. We find another DRF (but not Critical) in Lesueur – a eucalypt, *E. suberea*. Thirty to 40 plants in an inaccessible spot. Then the rare *E. megalosperma* – a small, bushy thing with big seed pods.

We find some in the 27,000 hectares of Lesueur National Park, but further north find another population pretty well seedless. A fire has been through and regeneration is slow. "With such a fire regime happening all the time, you are never sure whether they are going to reappear or disappear," says Sweedman.

Then, near Eneabba, *Eucalyptus impensa*. There are around 80 plants in existence.

We camp near Lake Indoon, in the darkening afternoon. Collections in the back of the four-wheel-drive, tied in a hessian sack. Amongst old trees that only grow around this strange and unexpected body of inland water. The next day we head into wheatlands to look for *Eucalyptus cuprea*. There are around 60 trees left, and we find some seedless, others isolated.

I get depressed. Even if they fenced them off, even if they tried to put a buffer between them and the chemical blitz of modern wheat production, I can't see that they are going anywhere. It looks pretty much over.

Does it matter?

Why does it matter?

Throughout the Quest, I remember words spoken to me years ago by Alan Danks, a Conservation and Land Management officer in Two People's Bay, on the South Coast of Western Australia. Danks has almost single-handedly pulled the noisy scrub bird back from extinction. There were only a handful, now there are hundreds. I asked Danks why he had devoted so much of his life to saving a bird that most of us will never see.

Because, he told me, it is important to know that it's there. Simple as that.

Important to our sense of morality and well-being. To our karma as a race, if you like.

Yes, I know I don't have to make a living out of modern wheat farming. I don't have to pay for the new tractor and the new harvesting header or pick up the huge super phosphate bill. I'm just a smart-arsed city bloke.

But I have stared extinction in the face and I can tell you one thing. It's just not damned good enough.

Patagonian Toothfish

WE ARE STANDING ON the ship's chain-smoky bridge talking about permaculture, the Icelandic skipper with the Scottish accent and I. The ship is running the Southern Ocean swell, drawing breath at the lip then plunging over the edge and gobbing out white either side. The air is filled with spume, blowing flat. Force five, he says. Perhaps six, I'd have expanded. Either way, for a patagonian toothfish boat, this is the equivalent of a hairdryer breathing over a backyard swimming pool. When you have green water rushing over the bow and up the foredeck and smacking into the wheelhouse, now that's when you've got a bit of Weather.

Fifty five degrees South. Maybe 54. Force 12 and up. Stop counting the wind speed at 60 knots. ("A hiding," as the skipper calls it.)

When the 88 metre Southern Champion is charging down breaking Antarctic swells longer than herself, and burying her bow

119

in the trough at the bottom, and you're trying to balance in the factory below, gutting fish and it smells like hell and it's colder than a fishmonger's slab ... well, then you're really patagonian toothfishing.

When, against the ever-present pulse of diesel engines, you're trying to eat your lunch at a 45 degree angle one way, then the other, then hold it down.

These have to be about the only fishers who don't have to tell Fishermen's Tales to make their exploits worth listening to. And neither does their prey. The patagonian toothfish – apart from being dark and ugly – is an awesome creature. It lives in deep, cold water in the sub Antarctic region. More than 4000km south-west of Albany (at the south-western tip of the Australian continent) at Macquarie Island and 2000km east of Hobart (on east coast of Tasmania), down near Heard Island.

Skipper Halli Stefansson and his crew have pulled them up from five metres, and from 2800 metres – where there is more than 250 times our normal atmosphere. They have been netted and dragged up alive from 700 metres, tagged and released for research purposes, just to swim straight back down. (They have no swim bladder to regulate their depth – they have evolved dense bones and an increased oil content, and the weight of these gives them neutral buoyancy.)

The discussion about the sustainable, permacultured principles Halli Stefansson practises on his New Zealand property is important, as is this reference to research, as are the two scientific observers on board and the nets of rubbish waiting to be lifted off the ship when she docks at Albany after a 46-day fishing stint (72 days if you count the shakedown trip from New Zealand on this inaugural voyage after a $3 million refit). The Southern Champion is fishing patagonian toothfish and icefish in a new fishery, and her owners Austral Fisheries, based in Perth, Western Australia, claim they are doing it right. Sustainably and with proper controls.

All of which is easy to say and good public relations – particularly when the fish stock you are aiming to exploit is in waters as sensitive as those of the sub Antarctic region. Frankly, as I jump from shark fisherman Geoff Cook's boat into an inflatable dinghy to be taken on board the Southern Champion, I'm acutely aware of this.

It is important to establish the relationship between our understanding of the fish stock, and the fish themselves, and the level of fishing. Should we be fishing a resource we don't know enough about? That's the question. But the legal fishing is bringing about a high level of research and understanding. They perhaps seem uncomfortable bedfellows.

But, as the World Wildlife Foundation itself has pointed out, 10 times the legal catch is taken illegally. David Carter, of Austral Fisheries, explains that without the legal fishing, and the knowledge that is coming from that, the fishery could be fished out illegally.

When a new stock is being fished, there is high investment, but the returns are good – the fishermen are taking their catches from a big existing biomass, there is a goldrush mentality. But, as the stock reduces, there comes the pressure of over-capitalisation, which means they fish harder into depleting stocks.

In addition, he says: "Commercial fishing is providing a reason for people to be interested in this area. Were it not for commercial fishing, Australian tenure to the area is zip.

"There are a lot of bad stories about fishing, so people develop the feeling that fishermen are not environmentally aware. That's not true." What they want is a reliable, sustainable resource, he says.

Skipper Stefansson himself admits fishing is a controversial business. It always has been, but is particularly so today. Some stocks are under pressure. Others are being fished out. Stefansson has been at sea since he was 15, and spent 17 years out in the weather fishing as a deckhand (which he misses). More importantly he also remembers, blow by blow, the Cod Wars between Iceland and the

UK in the 1970s, when gun boats came into play. He explains now: "Iceland could see that if it wasn't properly managed there would be nothing left." Perhaps it wasn't quite that simple, but all these events have helped to bring Halli to permaculture and the Southern Champion and her sistership, Austral Leader.

It is also a measure of his commitment to the cause of good fishing that he willingly swings the ship way off course to pick me up on their way home – adding an extra day to their nine-day steam back from the fishing grounds to Albany. It is a big gesture at the end of a long trip. Seamen aren't always known for their tact and diplomacy, and I'm prepared for some knocks from a crew kept away from family and pub. But nothing is said. (Well, not until they know me well enough to mention with surprisingly good humour that they'd have been home earlier, if it hadn't been for me). During our talks, they seem proud of the commitment to good fishing principles. "The cultural thing is important," says David Carter, back at Austral Fisheries. "And that pride and the sense of teamsmanship from two months in the freezer."

To establish the new fisheries, it is recognised that Austral Fisheries have created one of the world's most stringent environmental codes of practice for a commercial fishing operation. It was adopted by the Australian government and is now used as a statutory requirement for all permit holders fishing in the region.

Austral Fisheries' efforts were recognised in the inaugural WA Fishing Industry Council Commercial Fishing Awards, where they won two categories – the Michael Kailis Outstanding Commercial Fishing Industry Achiever of the Year and the Environment Award. The combination of these is a powerful endorsement of their methods and care.

In addition, Austral Fisheries initiated the formation of an international group called ISLOFICH – the International Southern Ocean Longline Fishing Information Clearing House. This group brought together organisations like the World Wildlife Fund, the Antarctic Southern Ocean Coalition, Greenpeace, Traffic

Oceania and a major media organisation to share information on illegal fishing and to lobby national governments to reduce this activity.

Austral Fisheries pressured the Australian Government to take decisive action against poachers, which resulted in the Australian navy arresting large foreign fishing vessels. On its last voyage, Southern Champion didn't see any poachers, says Stefansson. There are two types of poachers – old boats from South America and expensive boats from Scandinavia (mainly Norway), setting up to 30,000 hooks a day.

At a conference of the Commission for the Conservation of Antarctic Marine Living Resources, Australian Environment Minister Robert Hill strongly criticised the lack of protection for the patagonian toothfish. That criticism led to the conference accepting new measures against illegal fishing. Satellite-linked monitoring systems will be put on all licensed vessels and licensing and port access will be tightened.

The conference heard that between 60 and 90 per cent of the fish caught in the Southern Ocean are taken illegally, and some 100,000 sea birds are killed in the process.

Austral Fisheries' trawler Austral Leader pioneered the exploration of the sub Antarctic fisheries in 1994, at first fishing international waters. "She spent a long time in the wilderness trying to make a living. As we have seen with High Seas fish stocks all over the world, it's just a race to fish," says David Carter. "We lost a lot of money in the early days." So they set about leading the commercial development of the patagonian toothfish and icefish resources in the Australian Fishing Zone (around Macquarie and Heard islands). In 1998, the company was granted access for three years for a full program of trawl fishing.

We set off for an intimate tour of the Southern Champion. Halli wants me to see everything ... but everything. Every door is opened, every hatch lifted, every icy hold explored. There are no secrets.

Down in the fore and aft holds, stacked 5m deep by hand in minus 30C are 20kg sacks of patagonian toothfish ... headed, tailed, gutted and frozen on board. Four hundred tonnes in all – the last of the year's 3700 tonne quota (there was a 900 tonne quota of icefish). It is worth around $7.50 a kilo domestically. It is a premium fish – worth perhaps $22 to $24 on a fishmonger's slab in Australia and more when exported to its main overseas markets in Japan and the USA (some also goes to Chinese markets). In Japan, the delicate white flesh may be used for sushi or split long-ways and marinaded in soy, the rice pulp left over from saki making, and spices.

"This is the end of the year, so once we had got our quota, we just spent a week looking for icefish and then set for home," says Stefansson. "The icefish seem seasonal but the patagonian toothfish aren't."

Stefansson will fish in up to 55 knots of wind – "but it isn't easy". Especially on a pitching boat with an icy deck with huge nets to shoot off the stern. "And it depends on the bottom conditions. If it is a flat bottom and you know you are not going to get hooked up and you have a decent crew that isn't going to do anything stupid ..."

The Southern Champion carries a crew of 32, working eight-hour watches (eight on, eight off, through 24 hours a day, every day). It is a good, professional crew on this boat, says Stefansson. As is the crew on Austral Leader. Not going to do anything stupid. They are a mostly-tattooed mixture of sea hands, tough young deck guns, and factory workers. Half a dozen are Australian, many are New Zealanders. They are not seamen, but workers in the new, stainless steel heads-and-tails factory.

Among them are men like Jack Puru, a shearer who lives in Albany. A father of three, this is his first trip, and he spent the first four days crook as a yard dog that'd taken bait. But he still stood his watches at the conveyor belt processing fish. With the glint of the port's lights not far over the horizon, he says: "We had no experience, so we were lucky to get on. To have this opportunity."

The money's good, even for the processing and manufacturing hands. There's a retainer and then a share of the catch (being the last run of the season, the catch is smaller than usual, they say). No-one is clear what the cut-up will be, but they tell me they can earn $20,000 on a good trip. Captain Stefansson says a deckhand is likely to earn $40,000 to $50,000 a year. ("But that's totally reliant on catching fish.")

The nets are a giant funnel, like a sock. They have floats on the top and weights on the bottom, and otterboards are towed wide behind the boat to keep the mouth open. Two gates are opened at the ship's stern and the net is shot back into the ocean. The length of the cable towing it and the speed of the ship controls the depth. The net is trawled, maybe 500m deep, maybe for only 20 or 30 minutes, then hauled in. The end is opened and the catch floods down into the factory to be sorted, processed and frozen.

It is called "active fishing", where the fish are chased down. And it is incredibly accurate.

Through a combination of appropriate, 120mm mesh nets and fishing skill, the bycatch of other fish species is incredibly low. In fact, Stefansson says, the fishing is 99 per cent accurate to patagonian toothfish. Lynne Lever, working for Antarctic Division, but whose research is fully funded by Austral Fisheries, says that on this trip there has been only 0.5 per cent bycatch. "It is really, really unusual to have such a low figure." In fact, she says, it's unique. Some netloads have even been 100 per cent patagonian toothfish. The effect of bycatch was one of the fears at the start of fishing the region, she admits: "And there has been a lot of interest because it is the sub Antarctic and it's a new region — so lets get it right from the start."

She has collected data on more than 2000 patagonian toothfish and 800 icefish ... "what they eat, their sex, development, weight and length." This helps to build a database of information on the fish, which range from 70cm to 2m long. Some fish are tagged and released (one was caught three times). "We know hardly anything about the patagonian toothfish," explains Stefansson in his Icelandic-Scottish-Kiwi lilt. "They are a mystery species. But they are an amazing fish – incredibly hardy." They are omnivores, eating just about anything ... even the pig's trotter found in the stomach of one caught off Heard Island the previous year.

While Lynne Lever has concentrated on the fish, the other observer, Martin Scott of the Australian Fisheries Management Authority (also funded by Austral Fisheries), has concentrated on monitoring the interaction of gear with the environment.

"We are the eyes and ears of the fishery. I think we all realise this is one of our last chances to get it right," he explains. The crew has responded to this work, he says. They have started to take notice of the environment, the birdlife.

In four years, says the captain, only one elephant seal has swum into a net. On this trip, a fur seal was caught in a net, but released unharmed. "Originally there was opposition to us fishing at Macquarie Island. People thought we were down there killing birds and seals.

"From our point of view, it's important to have observers on board because no-one will believe us," says Stefansson, who is an avid reader of the history of the sub Antarctic –"such an unfortunate history of exploitation, when they first went down there. They laid places to waste and moved on.

"Although we take 3700 tonnes of fish a year, in the scheme of things it's only a small percentage. We try to minimise the impact. A big boat like this can do a lot of damage to the environment. But you don't have to ... it all comes down to respect."

All waste products from fishing are kept on board and they operate without the need for plastic strappings. Plastic waste and other non-biodegradeable material is stored for return to port and burnable waste is incinerated. Food scraps are also kept.

Martin Scott confirms the skipper's very high standards. "This is a developmental fishery, constantly evolving as issues come up. By the end of three years, when it becomes a commercial fishery, we will have all bases covered. And the fishing is also aiding research." In fact, 26 days of ship's time is donated for research each year, and the company has made a $150,000 contribution to research in the Macquarie Island fishery. The ship also undertakes biological and geological studies for the CSIRO and ADD.

The patagonian toothfish needs to be observed over a long period to see natural fluctuations and changes in stocks, says Halli Stefansson. "The last 200 years has seen much change in the sub Antarctic, with whaling and sealing. Things may still be in a state of flux."

A change of one degree in water temperature can have a great effect, with many fish dying of starvation. And scientists need to find out why the fish aggregate (shoal), whether for breeding, feeding or self-protection.

Chasing the patagonian toothfish is an expensive business. It costs $22,000 a day to run the Southern Champion, which was originally designed for fishing in Newfoundland. (After her previous owners failed to get fishing quotas, she lay idle in New Zealand for some years before her refit.) She uses nine tonnes of fuel a day to cruise at some 13 knots.

It's not a particularly big boat for the job, says the skipper. "The Russians have the biggest, up to 105m. But the ships need to be fairly manoeuvrable".

The crew are an optimistic bunch. That's part of the job, says Stefansson. "You HAVE to be incredibly optimistic. And have a reasonable faith in your own ability.

"I don't think of myself as separate from the crew. We are all just doing the some job on different parts of the boat. We are all links in the chain – if one part of the boat doesn't work, the boat doesn't work." So says the man the crew just calls Halli.

§   §   §   §   §

Halli Stefansson fetches a bundle of photographs to show me. Many are of his wife of more than 20 years, Virginia, a New Zealander whom he met when she was working in Iceland. Some are of his three daughters. Others are of the plaits those daughters insisted he had cut from his beard. There was a whole row of them, joining in a sort of bottom knot, hanging over his chest. They wouldn't be seen out with him.

But it is his property in New Zealand that he really wants me to see. "My wife really wanted to go back to New Zealand and I was keen to have a look. So we went there for Christmas in 1980 and I really liked the place." Then, in 1981, he bumped into a book by the guru of Australian permaculture, Bill Mollison, and was fascinated by it.

Now he believes "monoculture in any form is damaging." On his acres he has native bush – "forest for animals" – farmed trees, cows, sheep, chickens.

"Since I started fishing attitudes have chaned. Ten years ago there was a feeling the sea was inexhaustible. People have realised that's not the case. If you want to have a sustained fishery and not stuff up the ecosystem it has to be properly controlled.

"We are not in the situation where we can do what we like with the land or the sea. We have to take care of it. I would hate to think my kids couldn't go fishing."

The Eskimo Roll

THE BADGE IS A LITTLE MORE than 20 years old and has seen its share of water, much of it salty. Consequently, its once light-blue face is so speckled with rust you can only just make out its simple line drawing and few words. The drawing is a front-on view of a kayak. Sitting in it is a rather dorky, cartoon character man with a knitted hat, holding a paddle. It is no great artistic feat, but it has a twist. Both man and kayak are upside down. Beside them are the words: I CAN DO HALF AN ESKIMO ROLL.

I can't remember how, but I do know that the badge entered my life about the time I was learning to Eskimo roll a kayak. It was pinned, ceremoniously, to one of the pocket flaps of my expedition buoyancy jacket, and stayed there for many years, a perennial joke to be enjoyed by kayakers. It was only recently removed, along with sew-ons showing proficiency and qualification in kayaking's various disciplines, when I reached a point of not having to display them, or tell people.

It has left a rust mark.

The badge, of course, is in itself a statement that I can, in fact, successfully do a complete Eskimo roll – I suspect a person would only wear it if they could (if you couldn't, you would be unlikely to advertise the fact in kayaking circles).

When I hang upside down in the water, eyes tight shut to keep contact lenses in place, listening to the sounds of the waterworld, sinuses filling rapidly, I am confident that I will be able to roll up at will. Confidence is an important point. You can only really claim to be a "roller" when there is no doubt in your mind that you will pop back up. That it will work. This is the mental threshold that must be crossed.

It just happens one day. The vague, lingering doubt that you will, in fact, only just make it to the surface, where you will thrash around, gasping for air, doing a fair impression of drowning, before being sucked back down, simply vanishes.

It brings you into a secret covenant of mermen and mermaids who understand a strange, inverted world. When you sit in a kayak upside down, the surface remains the surface, only now it is silver, like liquid mercury, and the world as we know it – the air world – is viewed through this surface "film", which makes it surreal. It's like watching the familiar through that fine plastic film with which you cover food. And it has now become "the other world".

The world of your reality is the waterworld. That is what surrounds your senses. You are thinking and functioning properly, but your environment is water, and the air world is that strange place beneath you. You are sitting on its surface in your kayak, which fits so snugly and is so responsive that it has effectively turned the bottom half of your body into a float and made you a merman. Or mermaid.

Technically, Eskimo rolling a kayak is a combination of three vital physical manoeuvres ... a push to get the paddle to the surface, a large sweeping stroke which sculls across the surface of the water, giving enough lift to pull the upper part of the body upwards, and a hip flick strong enough to bring you to vertical. (The head must be the last part of the body to leave the water and the further back you lean, the easier it is.) If one element is missing, it is unlikely to work. Worse, if they are not all perfectly co-ordinated, it is unlikely to work.

Roy and Jane Farrance, who I have seen described as the parents of modern canoeing in Australia, wrote in their book This is Canoeing: "To learn, a paddler must learn part by part, and then string the individual parts together in one continuous, fluid movement." But they warn: "The Eskimo roll is the most complex canoeing skill of all."

Dennis Davis went further in his classic book, Canoeing: "I am not convinced that it is possible to teach yourself to roll from written instructions – although there have been some good attempts – so, apart from suggesting that you enrol for a course of rolling lessons, I do not propose going further into this aspect of canoeing." Perhaps a strange contradition for a tome published by Teach Yourself Books.

Be that as it may, it is good advice. Learning to roll is a hands-on business.

I had my first brief dip at it at Plas y Brenin, the United Kingdom's national mountain centre, in North Wales. The backdrop was splendid. The Welsh ranges lined the horizon, snow-capped. It was winter. The pool in which the rolling lesson was to be given was small and unheated – not much longer than the kayak itself and barely wide enough for the sweep stroke. (I remember being concerned, of all things, about knocking the tiles off the pool's edge with my wildly pitchforking paddle tip.)

What followed is all a bit of a blur. I recall someone once telling me that the head loses heat 94 times quicker than the body. I can verify this theory (if not the actual figure) by experience – turning upside down in that Welsh pool was rather like sliding into another dimension ... not even a sense of cold, more total disorientation. A state in which there is no thought and little reaction. Certainly no reasoning of how to turn this upside-down world back the right way up.

The lesson was all rather rushed. I had no ear plugs. No face mask. It was probably never going to work anyway. It certainly didn't fit with the Farrances' written advice: "The roller must be happy upside down, he must know where is up, where is down, which side is which, and be able to stay upside down for some time." The only one of these criteria I managed to fulfil was the last. I spent days with water rushing unheralded from my sinuses (a particularly sneaky eggcupful arriving over an immaculate white linen table cloth in a fancy restaurant), and put Eskimo rolling on the back burner.

Expedition paddler Jeff Gill has probably rolled a kayak more times than I have had hot dinners. A big-water veteran, he opened a teaching centre in Devon. It was there I first popped up, with Jeff patiently standing beside me, guiding the paddle, taking my body weight, until I finally got it right.

Eskimos have been rolling kayaks for many centuries, out of necessity. They hunted from kayaks (an Eskimo word) constructed from a frame and skins. The water was so cold that a quick, self-righting procedure was a matter of survival. You don't live for more than two or three minutes in those waters.

The British Canoe Union handbook reports that a missionary, in the 1765 book Birch Bark and Skin Canoes of North America, described 10 methods by which Eskimos righted their kayaks ... "the variation being by use of his full paddle, half a paddle, harpoon, until finally he would resort to hands only – although this, the writer observed, did not always work."

In 1927, an Austrian called Edi Pawlata became, reputedly, the first European to perform an Eskimo roll after studying the writings and descriptions of earlier explorers. In fact, he rolled by working the paddle through his hands until one was holding the blade of the paddle, giving much greater leverage. For this reason, the Pawlata roll is often still the first taught to beginners.

In 1930, an Englishman called Gino Watkins went to the Arctic surveying for a possible air route through the region. He was taught to roll by Eskimos before he went on kayak hunting expeditions with them. He needed the food for his survival. But the hunts led to his demise, and he died on a food-gathering trip.

An important part of the technique described by the 1765 missionary was the hip flick. But old film of people rolling, up until 1965, show kayakers sculling themselves to the surface with aggressive sweep strokes. Any movement of the hips came late in the piece, as a final movement to vertical.

The BCU says the "rediscovery" of the hip flick in 1965 revolutionised rolling. The Eskimo roll became a more familiar skill and, for some of us, a self-contained achievement, rather than a means to an end. Rather like the telemark turn in skiing.

There is a poetry to the synchronicity of the movements and a measured, controlled aggression to the final burst from the water (which, with experience, can be gradually diminished to a more languid, nonchalant movement).

There are hot days at my Australian home when I can happily spend a couple of hours in my swimming pool just rolling in a plastic kayak, face mask on, ear plugs in. Upside down, I feel comfortably removed from the world – hidden in my own secret, warm world of strange, resonant sound. Holding my breath for a long time, easily rolling up.

These moments underwater remind me of the time when I searched my own self-confidence and decided that I *could* roll. It was to do with walking taller, with a more relaxed gait and a straighter spine. Perhaps it was even, eventually, to do with writing essays like this, rather than the straight journalism I had been taught. (Rarely is one part of our lives not connected to the others.) It was a catalytic moment. Or, in truth, it was like a prolonged personal workshop, which produced more of a catalytic period than moment.

The transformation had more to do with self-reliance, self-understanding and self-belief than with holding a kayak paddle particularly so, flicking a hip with just the right attitude. It was also about conquering a fear of entrapment. These things have had wider implications in my life. Rolling a kayak, then, is both reminder and display of an ability to handle more important things.

For the technique of the final roll up, paddlers can chose any one of a number of Eskimo rolls.

The variety is extensive, but if you have three of them at your command, and can roll up either side of the kayak, you have all the artillery you need. With the screw roll, you just hold the paddle normally and roll. The Steyr roll starts from a lying-back position (sometimes useful in surf when you have been smashed onto the back deck). It can also be used if you lose your paddle, as you lie back and pick up half of the spare, split paddles mounted on the rear deck of a sea kayak. Re-entry and roll is the art of getting back into the boat when it's upside down, then rolling up.

If you have lost your paddles completely, there's the hand roll. Just rolling up, using your hands for the sweep stroke. Time seems to have stripped any hope of acquiring this art from me, but maturity has brought its own consolation. I always used to think hand rolling was the "ultimate" roll, but I now wonder what you'd do in a real-water situation – so dramatic it had ripped the paddle from you – were you to roll up by hand. Thrash on using your hands like a frenzied paddle steamer? It now seems to me quite useless, except as a party trick.

The Greenland roll, Kotzebue roll, Nunivak Island roll, storm roll (there are two recognised and named versions), King Island roll, put-across roll, Canadian screw roll, reverse screw roll, cross bow roll, hooked hand roll, and top hat roll and re-entry and roll are more matters of technical interest and exploration.

These are canvassed in Eskimo Rolling for Survival, by Derek Hutchinson, who shares the mantle of father of modern sea kayaking with Frank Goodman, designer of the Nordkapp in the 1970s for an expedition to North Cape in Norway. Hutchinson himself has designed a number of sea kayaks.

He quotes from Life with the Esquimaux by Captain Charles Francis Hall, written in 1864: "I enjoyed a rare sight. One of the Esquimaux turned summersets (sic) in the water seated in his kyak! (sic) Over and over his kyack (sic) went, till he cried 'Enough!' and yet he wet only his hands and face! This is a feat performed only by a few. It requires great skill and strength to do it. One miss in the stroke of the oar as they pass from the centre (when their head and body are under water) to the surface might terminate fatally. No one will attempt this feat, however, unless a companion kyak is near."

Paul Caffyn is probably the greatest adventure paddler of our time. He has paddled mostly-solo around Australia (which took almost a year), and solo around New Zealand (1500 nautical miles in 75 days), Japan and the United Kingdom (all on separate expeditions).

Rolling is rarely used, but a vital tool of the trade, he says.

Once you've got the philosophy and basic skills, you need practice. "Live practice". Not still-water practice where you line yourself nicely, prepare your paddle, set up in the correct position, then tip over comfortably into the water (on your favoured side). You need to do it for real. Do it in anger. Get knocked down and pop back up.

Farmer John played a big part in my further education. I was paddling mostly with members of the Advanced Sea Kayak Club in the UK at the time. Among the group was an electrician from the

London suburbs, a pig farmer of impressive intellect and general knowledge and Farmer John.

Farmer John (I can't recall his surname, if, indeed, I ever knew it) was in his mid-60s, barrel-chested, muscular, and hardened and tanned from a life outside, working the farm. He had only been paddling a couple of years, taking up canoeing as an outside interest as he eased the reins. He was a powerful man, headstrong in both manner and paddling – a balls-and-all, jump-in-there sort of guy. He feared neither whitewater nor surf. Neither rock nor reef. He had the total conviction in his own invincibility that leaves many of us with our teen years.

This makes a man a liability.

For a start, Farmer John had a habit of "dropping in". I don't mean a knock on the kitchen door revealing a cheery chap come to share a cup of morning tea. More a bloody-curdling Get-Out-The-Bleedin'-Way-I'm-Coming-In war cry as he dropped over the top of the wave you were happily surfing and right on top of you (the normal "rules" of surfing, that the first on the wave owns it, never applying, in his mind, to himself).

Farmer John really honed his fellow paddlers' rolling technique. He also broke a few of my ribs and, to this day, the severe ache from them often leads me to sleep in the recovery position.

Partly as a debt of gratitude for my own sense of satisfaction gained from the art of Eskimo rolling, partly because there is a sneaking enjoyment from being considered competent at a difficult practice, I have consistently taught others to roll over the past 20 years. It always takes three sessions. Always. And no-one has ever failed to master the basic screw roll, right side, which is all I undertake to teach.

I always hold the first two sessions in a swimming pool. There's something about being encircled by those walls that makes you feel safer. There are sides to hold onto while ducking down and hip-flicking up. And it's clean and blue and cheerful.

In my own pool, I have taught lawyers and sailors and writers and a mum-of-three who wanted to self-right her wave ski. The last was the most difficult. I had made the three session promise, but a wave ski is harder because the lateral balance is all wrong and you only have a lap belt for purchase on the craft (nothing to use your knees on). She, also, wasn't quite in the peak of fitness. But she cracked it, in three, and still writes to me from her now transitory home in the Philippines, Vietnam, the USA, to thank me. She doesn't paddle anymore. But she knows she can roll.

After learning the basic screw roll, further development of the art is a matter of personal interest, experimentation and dedication.

Workshopping underwater one day led me to a rather intriguing invention. Wouldn't it, I thought, be useful to have a dive air tank in circumstances such as these. So you could just hang around down there, virtually indefinitely, working things out.

Then it occurred to me that I was, in fact, sitting in one – I could sew tubing attached to a dive mouthpiece through the spray deck worn around the waist and clipped over the boat's coaming.

The question of making this entry point waterproof has never been completely solved, so the time the "tank" would last is not indefinite.

The idea just needs refining, I have been telling myself for a decade. But the theory is good.

Last Sunday morning I had a nice paddle with a friend to some islands about five nautical miles off the Australian coast. We left early, spotted three or four particularly interesting birds, had an early breakfast on one of the islands, then paddled on. By the time we turned for home, the sea breeze was already in, at a good 20 knots. The sea breeze on the west coast of Australia starts literally as if someone has flicked a switch. Whitecaps come with it. The water streaks, the tops of the swell break. It was going to hit us on the beam (the side of the boat) all the way home ... not a comfortable or stable proposition.

Half way home my paddling companion caught a wave and rode it 300 metres, away from me. I was meditating on the colour of the water − a turquoise underlaid by royal blue, so deep it was textural, three dimensional. Between the meditation and catching him out of the corner of my eye, I missed a freak wave coming my way. It broke over me and, embarrassingly, knocked me over. I rolled up. My paddling companion never even knew.

Just Cruising

THE LOBBY IS FLANKED by a pair of lifesize dolphins leaping at identical angles from the bubbling waters of a pool. The pool is landscaped with river rocks, and there is a sequence of fountains, all carefully lit.

Built over the pool of water is a Chinese temple, with much red and gold, up steps which have pinprick lights outlining their curved contours. Behind it, three glass elevators (outlined by more pinprick lights) whisk people up and down five storeys.

The lobby floor is of a highly polished, highly reflective, imitation black marble, which matches the black marble columns around its edge. Look up and there is a rim of shops and, higher, a large number of black "mirrored" windows, against apparently sandstone walls.

Around the edge, there's a flotilla of armchairs and solid

couches of various colours of velour. Wood panelling. A grand piano plays Tie a Yellow Ribbon Round the Old Oak Tree without human intervention, its footpedals moving too. There is a carpet with a bold, gold, traditional Asian pattern, which looks particularly odd against the massive circular rug of contemporary pastels (mostly turquoise), with underwater motifs. The rug looks like some take-home from a Barrier Reef gift shop (I am later told that when the designer bought it for $28,000 everyone thought he was mad. But now it's in place, they are quite happy with it).

On top of it is a rather grand, heavy timber table with delicately curved feet, supporting a massive flower arrangement.

I reach over and tap a dolphin. It echoes. Hollow. Fibreglass. I tap one of the black marble columns. Fake too.

Things ain't what they seem to be.

In fact, the whole of the mega cruise vessel SuperStar Leo is a mix of theme park and Dream Ship. It is there to satisfy expectations of opulence and luxury – and if it can do it in one room, so much the better. Traditional China, Rome, England and a Parisian showroom in one sweep of the eye.

This international theme is also reflected by the immaculate crew lined up behind the reception desk. Each wears an immaculate badge with their name and, under this, the name of the country they come from. In this case China, Malaysia, Finland, Philippines; the mix completely in keeping with the multicultural decor of this Disney on (Melted) Ice ship.

The 268 metre long, $350 million SuperStar Leo – the first cruising megaship in Asia – is built to carry 2800 passengers. Each week this block-of-flats-with-a-pointy-end voyages out of Singapore on a two-day and a five-day cruise. There are only 1500 on board for this two day voyage, but added to 1100 crew, that's still 2600 people on one ship.

Leaving the piano chirpily completing a Bee Gees repertoire, I set out to find them. We boarded on Friday and by now – early on day two – this has become something of a hobby. I'm starting to think SuperStar Leo is a Ghost Ship. It is a 76,800 tonne whale of a thing with a special talent for swallowing people.

I set off down a corridor lined by lifesize ancient Chinese warriors and traditional birds-and-flowers wall panels and end up at Henry the Black, an English-style pub. I look through the window. Nah. Dead as ... well, dead as an English pub.

I head out to the stairs and lifts, surely an area of activity. A cleaner (Philippines. Immaculate) stops his vacuum cleaning to bow and wish me good morning. This is encouraging. I head down the stairs, past a sandstone figure ("Thailand, reminiscent of Baphuon style, Angkor Period"). No-one there. So I head back up, past a terracotta relief ("India, two goddesses") to the seventh floor deck. Round the corner, the Moulin Rouge, a largely pink, 1000-seat showroom (with revolving stage and the scene of an occasional White Tiger show) is empty. So too the Tai Pan Restaurant and Maharajah's casino. No-one hanging round in Maxim's upmarket French restaurant.

Up past the head of a deity ("Burma, reminiscent of Banteay Srei style, 11th Century") and a quick lap past the Shogun Japanese restaurant before heading to deck nine, past a hunting scene ("Indonesia, terracotta relief"). This is a cabin deck, and I bump into half a dozen people in the corridors and occasionally hear the heavily muffled sound of a TV behind a porthole styled door, complete with a large fan shell holding its number.

This lifts my spirits again.

Up past the bronze warrior ("Cambodia, reminiscent Angkor Period") and a sandstone figure of Vishnu ("Vietnam, reminiscent Kompong Preah style, pre-Angkor Period").

I pass the Raffles buffet and somehow burst out through a door into the midst of the Tivoli Pool area, complete with more Roman columns (fake) and cornices (fake) than are positively decent, a swimming pool with a tiled patterned bottom, and four spas.

I walk up a few steps to the German Bier Garten and see a handful of men around a table, either starting early or still going from the night before.

No-one in the gym. Not a soul on the golf driving range. The basketball court is a barren wasteland.

Then I find them. Well, 11 of them to be exact – six playing table tennis, two watching and three kids in the Buccaneer's Wet and Wild pool (complete with fake rocks with backlit, inset jewels which mysteriously, and quite enchantingly, continually change colour).

You can put the apparent absence of people on this Ghost Ship down to one thing. SuperStar Leo's layout. She's a Tardis – or, at least, she spreads people super-effectively through her extensive bulk. The biggest passenger ship ever built specifically for the multi-billion dollar Asian and Pacific market, she was constructed by Meyer Werft to their faultless German standards and came into commission late in 1998. The interior was styled by Robert Tillberg's Swedish-based Tillberg Design.

Well, that's the tour of the public areas of the 13-decked Dream Ship. But don't ask me to repeat it. Despite carrying the map of the 10 public decks in our backpockets, I don't think any of the Australian contingent on this trip really mastered navigation (the Scandinavian officers who run the Working Ship behind this Dream Ship did rather better as we cruised down the busy high-way of the Strait of Malacca and back.)

Cruising is about running away. It is about the wide, washing-machine of a wake, about islands passing in the steamy mist, about milky water washing down the sides of the ship. It is about leaving things behind.

You could stay in a comparably luxurious resort in Asia and have all the facilities you have here. Bars, restaurants, pools. But you wouldn't have the motion. The sense of movement. Of travelling. Of going somewhere. Or, perhaps even more interestingly – and, unlike its heritage of going-somewhere cruiseline predecessors – in this case of going nowhere in particular, except back to where you started. Of moving for the sake of moving.

It brings an instant isolation from everyday life, and a chance to leave your everyday self somewhere behind, on dry land. Which is what two of the Australian contingent, in particular, are doing now, in the early hours of the morning, dancing to the band Boney M, who have knocked out some very good versions of Bob Marley songs and are now into Eric Clapton's I Shot the Sheriff.

The two Australians are dancing in a particularly seductive manner and one is repeatedly telling the other: "I love you. I love you." He has already told everyone else within kissing distance – female, male, friend, stranger, passing waitpersons etc – precisely the same thing. He's just in a sort of loving mood this evening. His dance partner – in this case male – seems oblivious to the compliment.

Boney M had just come up for a quick rehearsal session by Tivoli Pool, but the Australian contingent had flocked from the German Bier Garten to dance poolside. Many people of other nationalities are drawn by the music, but lurk at a safe distance. The evening session goes on until two-ish, I think, before Boney M unplugs.

The Australian contingent then adjourns to the disco to be strobed, disco-balled, spotlighted and blasted with bad, too-loud music for several more hours. Once again people of other nationalities sit in the shadows, but most are eventually pulled – yes, physically pulled by the hand – from their seats and into the fray.

"OK Aussie. OK." The girls are shy, in that particularly controlled Singaporean way, until they hit the dance floor. Then they go beserk.

The Aussies are doing their bit for multiculturalism and world peace, alright. And the next night the initiative is repaid. It had started with four of the Australian contingent having a pleasant beer in Henry the Black's, that English-style pub. A handful of Singaporeans sat around the edge, a circle of Westerners were enjoying a quiet drink.

Then Jimmy, the bar's resident singer, working alone on a classical acoustic guitar, broke from a string of Neil Diamond numbers into that tune from Top Gun. You know the one. Where Tom Cruise and Goose sing at the piano with air-mikes.

Well, that was it really.

The Australian contingent broke into song, one of them kicking in with a harmonising accompaniment knocked out with cocktail stirrers on various part-empty glasses, the other bongo-ing on a counter. It was on. Before you knew it they were dancing (the circle enjoying a quiet drink quickly left), and every Singaporean in the house was drawn into the mellee, particularly a youngster called Aaron, who had been living in Australia and has gel-spiked hair and a particularly unusual sort-of-swimming hand movement on the dance floor.

Jimmy, thrilled by the response, just rolls from one number into the next without missing a note, while Aaron's grandad sits in the corner, harmonising, and occasionally taking the lead, on the karaoke microphone.

I conclude a particularly nasal rendition of Time In a Bottle, which happens to be one of only two songs ever written in my key (the other is that number that Maverick and Goose sing at the piano).

Then, somewhere around 1am, I think, Aaron's grandad eases himself from his window bench seat in the corner and stands, speaking into the microphone. Jimmy pauses. Grandad stops the party dead. "I would like to say something to all the Australians," he says. (Oh no, are we in trouble again?)

"To all our Australian friends. I would like to thank them for what Australia did for us in the war. If they hadn't we would all be speaking Japanese now. They came and they fought for us, and I

144

would like to thank them."

He solemnly works his way round the group, shaking the hand of each. Then he leads Jimmy in a rendition of Waltzing Matilda.

Grandad has re-established our shared history, and with it our connection. (It reminds me of Aboriginal groups, when they meet at gatherings, sitting under trees, retracing their family connections.) History joins us.

We roll on through a couple more Aussie classics which, to our combined embarrassment, we know few of the words of.

Then it's over.
Then it's the disco.
Then it's dawn.

Behind the Dream Ship is the Working Ship. You open fancy-finished doors in well-carpeted hallways and step through into another world – to the Working Ship's plain-painted walls and practical floors. A ship that looks like a ship, not an hotel.

Let me share some numbers. There are 4686 beds, 250,000 square meters of insulation, 8000 kilometers of wiring, 1800 toilets, 40,000 light fixtures, 8000 life jackets, 18 lifeboats, 50 life rafts. Some 1800 tonnes of freshwater can be produced daily from seawater, and up to 2500 tonnes stored. She can carry 2600 tonnes of fuel oil. There are 11 public elevators, eight crew elevators.

There are 1843 dining chairs, 323 tables, 42,000 glasses.

Executive sous chef Mike Byers ("New Zealand") says up to 10,000 meals a day are prepared by his 150 cooks for the 10 food outlets and crew mess. He shows me a steam kettle holding up to 200 litres, woks big enough to bath in. They can spend $300,000 a trip on food provisions alone.

There are 450 fire doors, 6500 fire alarm sensors, 6000 sprinklers, and 44 watertight doors, one of which is sliding closed behind us now. Staff chief engineer Lars Garte ("Norway") has led us deep into the working bowels of the ship – down companion-ways, through bulkhead doors.

(I have been dying to ask someone what would happen if this cruise liner hit an iceberg but Lars Garte, despite his twinkly little half-smile, is too serious a man for this.)

There are four 18-cylinder diesel MAN engines, but these are not what directly drive the ship's two massive propellers. They generate electricity, for electrical motors which can turn the propeller shafts anything between one and 145 revolutions a minute, allowing the Leo to cruise at a comfortable 15 knots and giving her a top speed of 25 knots (very quick for a boat this size and, allegedly second only to the QEII which, although built in 1969, was built for speed). It takes about 20 minutes to accelerate from standing to top speed and two nautical miles to stop.

There are four massive air conditioners (each of 4500 kilowatts) and waste management systems that individually grind glass, met-als and plastics for return to shore for recycling; compress and drain wet waste (so that the dry residue can be burnt), and incinerate paper and cardboard. Sewerage is drawn down through a vacuum system before being treated and discharged. Everything complies with the highest world standards.

There are 40 engineering staff, but the ship can be run by two down here in the guts and one up in the control room – surround-ed by computer screens, with buttons to open and shut valves, turn things on and off, run the whole show. At the moment there are three and they look rather bored.

Down in the ship's belly there is noise.
Down in the ship's belly there is a wet heat.
Down in the ship's belly there is the smell of lubricant.

In the disco, the smell is almost identical. The noise is an interminable disco mix, with plenty of Bee Gees and Grease numbers. The wet heat is from bodies. The lubricant comes in glasses, handed over the bar (and paid for through a plastic card system on this money-less ship).

I have spent some time working on the science of the cruising equation. I have come up with what I believe to be a fairly defensible mathematical equation:

Protein + electricity + salt water + alcohol = pheromone.

To cut to the chase, there is a lot of talk about sex. There's a lot of eyeing up, a lot of flirting. There's a helluva lot of hard work being done by some individuals on others. And a helluva lot of dodging going on. There's plotting. There's planning. There's an ocean of mindless conversation, endured in the name of foreplay.

At breakfast there are quite obvious lies about conquests, and equally obvious lies about lonely nights. There are less tasteless (but far more entertaining) allegations about those not present. There are allegations of photographs to support allegations. There are allegedly misleading photographs which allegedly support allegations but which, in truth, are allusives.

It's exhausting.

I just spend my time trying to work out what to wear. This is my first time on a luxury cruise ship – I have packed everything from a finely cut English pure wool reefer jacket, with white shirt and nautical tie, to the few clothes I possess which I would class as "resort". I even bought a pair of loafers.

Nevertheless, it seems that every time someone knocks on my door to "pick me up" on the way to some gathering, what I am wearing doesn't match what they are. So I make some excuse and duck in to change, hoping they won't notice that I reappear 30 seconds later in completely different attire. Inevitably they do.

There are times in your life which pass too quickly, times which pass too slowly. Times when time itself doesn't seem to be functioning normally. When 20 minutes in a deckchair musing the ocean seems to take half a day, when you dance briefly by a pool then find it's 2.30am.

There are times to treasure. Times to keep locked inside you. Jim Croce sang that there never seems to be enough time to do the things you want to do, once you find them. Chances are he never went cruising.

§   §   §   §   §

On our last night on the SuperStar Leo, we watch dolphins jumping from the water at the bow of a huge passing cargo ship. In pairs. In threes. Right by her big bulb of a bow.

As we approach Singapore, I count 50 more cargo ships at anchor. A strange car park if ever there was one.

This strangeness is just part of the strangeness of arrival – of an ending, and resumption, of time. There is a real sense of home-coming.

We haven't been far, but we've been at sea.

Smart Casual

IN THE YEAR 249, at a special celebration of the millennium of the founding of Rome, 1000 pairs of gladiators entered the arena of the Colosseum in Rome and paraded in a lap of honour. They halted before the Emperor: "Ave, Imperator, morituri te salutant." Hail, Emperor, those who are about to die salute thee. Then they engaged in combat.

There are no figures as to how many did, in fact, die. But what is known is that 32 elephants, more than 50 lions, 12 tigers, and six hippopotamuses died, all sent in from the provinces of the Roman Empire. The slaughter lasted from dawn until dusk and the arena was awash in blood.

Between AD80, when the Colosseum was inaugurated by Emperor Titus, and the 6th Century, when animal fighting was banned, some 5000 animals died. (Gladiatorial duels were forbidden in AD404 by Emperor Honorius.)

As we know, the Colosseum still stands, monument and tourist attraction, with only vague echoes of the 50,000 people who watched the slaughter. They bought tickets and entered through doors marked with the number on their ticket, just as audiences around the world still do today. They watched according to rank – from the 5000 slaves standing on the terraces to the 45,000 seated, rising higher up the elaborate structure according to their status. Some, dressed in finery, sat on marble benches.

The gladiators dressed in purple and gold. It was a spectacle.

We were approaching the next millennium celebration when I received an invitation to a modern-day Colosseum. A structure so close to the original that it's almost eerie – oval, terraced, rising in rank, with VIP boxes, accommodating almost exactly the same number of spectators. And the spectacle – modern-day gladiators pitched in physical combat for our pleasure, running out through their banners, sculptural.

But today, dressed in blue and gold. The colours of this modern Australian Rules football club. And the invitation? To sit in the President's box. To sit with the Emperor and watch the combat from the elitist and luxurious eyrie.

The invitation comes with two words at the bottom. The dress code. Smart Casual. I ring to accept. "Oh, and Ian. What should I wear?" Something relaxed, he says. "Just a jacket and tie." Just a jacket and tie? Pushing through a footy crowd crammed outside the turnstiles while wearing a jacket and tie will, in itself, be an enlightening experience.

The room is midway down one of the longest sides of the oval. In exactly the same position as the Emperor's suite at the Colosseum (his was on the north side, the Prefect of Rome had his on the south side). But the actual room doesn't live up to its name. It's just a room with washable carpet and grey walls and not very comfortable dining chairs. A room with high television sets slung around the ceiling so you can follow what is happening in other matches, which may have some bearing on the team's position on the ladder.

However, the room's position is unassailable. It sits high up, and the reserved seats outside have cushions and outdoor carpet is laid over the concrete floor. This is luxury indeed.

The food in the President's room is delicious. Two fine steaks wrapped in bacon, a neat little bundle of asparagus, a nice glob of mashed potato. The wines, beyond reproach. During this, banter from the regulars and polite conversation from the guests breaks off, and the club's most senior officials have their say.

I feel I am being let in on a very special secret. Expect to finish between fourth and tenth on the ladder this year, said the chairman. This is not a failure – this is a plan. This is part of building for the future. This is part of being a young team, and not just buying in old hands to prop up immediate success.

All very enlightening stuff.

Then we are invited to wander outside and actually watch the game. The queue is immediate, orderly and urgent – not at all what I had expected. And what had I expected? Well, from the conviviality of the room, I had expected people to be slow, even reticent, to actually go and watch the footy. But, not at all. This is a footy crowd.

Australian Rules Football deserves careful (if brief) description. Various friends speak of it disparagingly. "How can you call a bunch of blokes chasing a rugby ball round a cricket pitch Football?"

"It's like watching a bowl of spaghetti wriggling."

In truth it is the most athletic and skilful of games. The ball may be kicked or handpassed ("punched" with hand closed, fist-like) in any direction. A player is awarded a Mark when he catches a longer kick. He is then awarded a set kick.

There are four goalposts – two taller ones in the middle through which goals worth six points are scored, one shorter "behind" post either side through which single points are scored.

Accuracy is rewarded. It is a fast and physical game. Tough. It is a man's game. A wingman may sprint 20km during a game of four 30-minute quarters. He may be continually harassed and abused. He may suffer an all-too-common cruciate ligament knee injury and be "out" for a year. But that's footy, and it's a gladiator's life.

Above all it is theatre. It stimulates a sense of community. The ground is a cathedral. Built and then continually further developed post-war, when few comparable religious cathedrals have been built.

§   §   §   §   §

Over more than 20 years as journalist and writer, I have become unselfconscious in asking what to wear. Indeed, an early lecturer told me I needed to equip myself with only two things to be successful in journalism: an ability to listen and a comprehensive wardrobe.

It wasn't bad advice. In fact, I now advise people to "listen and understand". But I go along with the wardrobe. Generally there isn't much time to "get along" with people. You rarely have much time to build a relationship strong enough to encourage them – or at least give them confidence – to talk to you. To trust you. To know you well enough to feel they can confide.

If you arrive on a cattle station wearing a floral shirt and a pair of boardshorts (or, worse still, a sheep-farmer's hat), chances are they will think you're an idiot. It's a long way back from there. If you arrive on a prawning boat in the Gulf of Carpentaria in a neatly laundered pair of white pants and a smart shirt (rather than the customary "Stubbies" shorts, ripped t-shirt and thongs on your feet), the same.

Even for the recent launch of a new motorcycle, I asked what sort of route the test ride would be – fast or cruising? – and what sort of riding gear the others were likely to wear.

Tonight, at the footy, the jacket and tie are pretty much   perfect. Not too formal, but a jacket and tie nevertheless. Both Italian, the dark jacket "soft cut", the tie not overbearing. Worn over a black shirt.

The Media

IF YOU COULD HEAR the guts of the building, you would be deafened by the scream of a million words squeezing down cables together. E-mails, faxes, Internet, networked messages, library systems, incoming news services, and a flow of articles being filed. All garbled. Running at incredible speed.

What you can hear is the incessant tapping of keyboards at 200 computer terminals, in an office the size of a sports field. A modern newsroom with virtually no pillars and no partitions. Blinds permanently down to filter out natural light, as it flares across computer screens, making words invisible. And over it, the hum of phones and one-sided conversations. TV sets nattering news, hoarse with racing, or merely miming.

The buzz of the building, the whizz of terminals, click of keyboards, combine in a crazy concerto.

In a drawer beside her, the young journalist keeps a clean manila envelope. Sometimes she sees it, and knows that inside are the big degree credentials that have put her here. And on top of the envelope is an old paperback with yellowed pages and turned down corners, about some old hack journo.

And sometimes, amongst all the static, she feels herself drift off and dream …

§   §   §   §   §

Barlow blew smoke, and watched it loop into a ring in the cold air. He stuck the cigarette back in the corner of his mouth, where he liked to wear it. He shrugged deeper into the tall collar of his coat and turned into an alleyway, his steel caps striking flinted notes off the walls.

He stopped at the end, under a lamp. The rain drops on his shoulders sparkled like stars, then shone pink as he stood under the Daddy Long Legs club's red neon lights. The long legs kicked a can-can. Corny but cute. He dropped the cigarette and ground it into a muddy puddle. Then he stepped quickly down the three steps into the club.

It was just the way he thought it would be. Dark, sleazy and smoky. Girls were dancing on a makeshift stage, their skimpy beaded triangles at face-height. They didn't look convinced, but the punters weren't there to look at their expressions. They sat, mostly alone, at tables covered with empty glasses. Some looked around as he went straight to the bar and ordered a double whisky. No ice. The barman stood slowly wiping a glass with a dirty cloth. He stopped to pour the whisky, eyeing Barlow suspiciously.

Barlow got straight to the point. "Know a Ned Clover?"

"Who's askin'?"

"Let's just say it's business. Now, do you know him?"

"I ain't saying I do, and I ain't saying I don't."

"Well you'd better say something, and quick."

Barlow's voice was sharp as a knife. He saw the barman ease away. Twenty years of experience told him that wouldn't work. He went for the wallet in his inside pocket. Gently, though. He didn't want to spook him. He looked around and slid a fifty on to the damp bar.

The barman spoke this language. "It's more likely I do than I don't." He was going to play it coy. One side of Barlow's mouth lifted to a half-smile. He couldn't help liking a good dealer. He slid another fifty on to the bar. "That help the part that Likely Do?"

The barman could read it right. A hundred was the limit. He stuck the notes deep and sticky in his pocket. "He left 'bout half an hour ago. Went down the Laravee Club. He'll still be there. Tall guy, leather jacket, scar. You won't miss him."

Without a word, Barlow turned away from the bar and started to pull up his collar.

"Anyway, who's askin'?" said the barman, braver and louder.

Barlow froze. Slowly turned. "Barlow. From the City Reporter."

The barman stiffened. Yes, he'd heard of Barlow, that tough old hack from the City Reporter. Everyone had. He'd stuck his foot in a few doors round this town on the way to a story. (And everyone knew he didn't care what he had to do to get it.) Made up a few up too, they reckoned.

The barman was glad for the hundred, and glad to see Barlow heading for the door ..."

§   §   §   §   §

The phone rang, drawing the young journalist back to the techno-logical cacophony. "Hi, it's Annie here from A2Z Public Relations. I just wanted to make sure you got the press release I faxed to you this morning."

Yes, she had. She wanted to get rid of her as soon as possible. But Annie wanted to know if she needed any more information. (If she did, she thought, she'd buy a cigarette and wait for a rainy night.) She turned back to her report – a modern journalist, buried under the rubble of the last decade's explosion in the public relations and marketing industries.

It is just part of the rock symphony of modern media. In Australia, people aged over 14 already watch television for an average 21 hours a week and listen to radio for 16. Three million people use the Internet at least once a week and more than six million occasionally. More than 3200 pages are produced by metropolitan newspapers and newspaper magazines each weekend alone – 1300 of them "entertainment" pages.

Worldwide, the conundrum for the media has always been striking the right mix of information and entertainment – and increasingly the balance has swung towards entertainment. Readers don't want a diet of pure, dry information.

Readers and listeners ... now called Consumers in the Language of Product ... have been educated by the snappy sound bite. They have been cajoled by colour, titillated by talkback.

And society in Australia – like societies everywhere – gets the media it deserves. Talkback is there because it is commercially viable. Each edition of Woman's Weekly sells some 805,000 copies, Woman's Day some 660,000 copies, New Idea 483,000, Who Weekly 201,000 and the Bulletin 75,000 (oh, and Teletubbies magazine 43,000).

On television, World's Wildest Police Videos rates its head off.

"Consumers" drive the media. What we won't listen to, won't watch, won't read – won't wear – generally won't happen (or, it won't happen for long).

Only one publication in the world bought and ran the photo-graph of Sophie Rhys-Jones' breast popping out – and then The Sun in London apologised. Why? Because their readers wouldn't wear it. If the newspaper management hadn't thought there would be a backlash in terms of circulation, would they have apologised?

Senior journalists are aware that they work for the readers, and daily newsroom conversation centres around what is relevant for the readership, what they will want to read. Media organisations are businesses that rely on the public's support.

And where does the journalist sit in this mass of media? At the start? In the middle? Perhaps, increasingly, at the end.

As the forms of delivery multiply, and the amount of the mate-rial they carry rises commensurately, journalists will be increasing-ly important in filtering, editing and interpreting. Some of us (the more arrogant perhaps) would even see our role as trying to help people make sense of the world – not just offering them a descrip-tion of it.

The modern journalist is a highly qualified, technologically lit-erate, often office-bound entity. Journalists today work for slimmed-down, manpower-efficient business organisations. They don't sit round smoky old bars snouting out story leads, they most-ly sit on the end of faxes and e-mail, part of a process swinging away from news gathering to news processing.

The Mac has long been an important tool for journalists – only once it was a grubby raincoat. I look around my office and I can't see a Barlow among them. Barlow did exist and I knew him and his mates, and I even worked with him, but it wasn't here, and if there are one or two left, they are dinosaurs way down the path toward extinction. I was there for the initial breakup of London's Fleet Street in the early 1980s, when everything started to change. I wasn't there for the death of Princess Diana, but that was when the readers (with their thirst for coverage) and the media (with their desperation to supply it) knew they had gone too far.

The public does have standards and expectations – and it bucks when it believes they have been ignored or broken. If there is any doubt of industry and public concerns, you need only look at the discussion over Internet censorship legislation and the survival of public broadcasters.

Add to that public concern over the distribution of media ownership. Readers, watchers and listeners want truth, fact, unbiased comment.

The sort of debates which have surrounded the functions of the media in recent years are the sorts of debates that must be directed to any institution of power. As the power of the media continues to grow – the more pervasive the messages, the more the messages saturate and shape a culture – this process of questioning can be expected to go on.

Like police, teachers and other influential groups caught in the shifting currents of society, the media has been through, and will continue to go through, a period of turbulence and adjustment to changing roles and circumstance. It is a time for ethical, organisational, legislative and philosophical questioning.

If you polled today, newspaper journalists would probably come out as badly as ever. A recent Morgan poll in Australia showed that only nine per cent of people believed and trusted them. Under used car salesmen. Under estate agents. Under politicians. Under television journalists. Under everyone, actually. (Although, interestingly, this figure had risen from seven per cent.)

Barlow has passed into myth, yet somehow part of him is still alive. Perhaps we all need that image. Perhaps readers and journalists like the romance of it. Journalism has moved on, but the polls show that the popular impression of the journalist as rogue hasn't moved on with it.

Why are newspaper journalists so unloved?

Readers' views are still coloured by the antics of the European paparazzi, by the notion of chequebook journalism, by the fear that there are agendas running behind the scenes. Yet these are generally absent in Australia – or, when they do occur, are carried out in response to reader demand.

Why are newspaper journalists so unloved? At some point, readers have to ask themselves.

§   §   §   §   §

Barlow was on to something. Ned Clover had given him names and phone numbers. Eventually. Under flickering city lights, he walked back to the office through the rain. Sirens wailed over the east end of the city, pricking his instincts.

He walked through a crowd heading home after a night out. They were drunk and silly. A girl draped a streamer round his wet neck, but he pushed her away. He didn't think of his own loneliness. He didn't think of this as work. He was just doing what had to be done. He slipped out his hip flask and bit at the whisky.

He walked up the back stairs of the office. This way you could smell the printers' ink. Sometimes, earlier than this, you could feel the presses shake the building. But not tonight. He looked at his watch – 2.30am. Everything was off the press by now.

He opened the door and stepped into the office. There were virtually no pillars, and no partitions. Just 200 computer terminals. He could hear the guts of the building screaming a million words at once. The buzz of the building, the whizz of terminals, the click of keyboards, combined in a crazy concerto.

And a girl on late shift reading a paperback with yellowed pages.

Barlow knew he had come to the wrong place. He turned and stepped back through the door, danced fast down the stairs and back on to the dirty streets …

The author would like to thank:
Angela Wellington for her faith and editing;
Virginia Ward for her confidence and encouragement;
Family and friends for their patience and endurance;

West Australian Newspapers, where he is a member of
The Writers' Group and an editorial executive, for its
opportunities and practical support. Particular thanks to the
Editor, Paul Murray, and Sundry Publications Manager,
Simon Waight. Some of these essays have been published
previously in West Australian Newspapers publications.

The author would also like to acknowledge the help of all those
featured in these essays, and others who made them possible.

The author acknowledges that memories of events differ.
"This is how it seemed to me."

Stephen Scourfield has been a writer and photojournalist for more than 20 years.

He has edited many newspapers and magazines.

Born in England, he emigrated to Australia in 1985. He is now a proud Australian and spends much time travelling the continent's remote places.

He is currently working on his next two books.